Talk Early, Talk Often

Why families need to have ongoing conversations about human trafficking and technology

Stephanie Olson

First Edition published by The Set Me Free Project 2026

This book is intended for educational and informational purposes only. The topics discussed may feel sensitive or activating for some readers. Please take care of yourself as you read pause when needed, skip sections if necessary, and seek support from a qualified professional if you find that difficult

First Edition

Contents

CHAPTER 1

What is human trafficking?

> ***You may choose to look the other way, but you can never again say you did not know.***
>
> ***~William Wilberforce***

There's an attack happening on our kids as we speak. And this attack, well, it isn't happening where you might think it's happening. It's in our own homes. Every day, our youth and young adults (actually, even old folks like me) are targeted online by people wanting to do harm. This has never been more prevalent than it is today, largely because of social media sites and gaming platforms.

I am in no way saying that social media and gaming are bad or evil. No. In fact, these can be great tools for so many things. Social media can make a large world feel much smaller. We can keep in touch with family members who have moved across the globe. We can promote our businesses without paying a dime. Users can find inspiration for the day at the click of a button. Social media can be a wonderful thing. But as with everything that is wonderful, there are negatives and consequences that can go along with it. Let's remember that when we have access to the world, the world has access to us. It's that simple. And to top it off, because this world is on a device that we can easily put in our pockets, we can take it anywhere. That's convenience, right? But it is just as convenient for those who want to do us harm. Many social media platforms have an age restriction of 13 years old. But the current sign-up process is so lacking that anyone can enter a birthday into the registration form and create an anonymous profile. The problem is compounded when social media companies like Meta plan on creating new versions of their social media sites targeted specifically at kids as young as six years old. Facebook, Instagram, Messenger, WhatsApp, and Meta Horizon are all properties of the infamous Mark Zuckerberg's company, Meta.[1] And with the recent Facebook whistle-blower scandal, we learned that social media companies can intentionally choose profit over the well-being of their patrons.[2] So, as parents and caregivers, what are we to do to help our children stay safe online?

Human trafficking: What is it, and why should I care?

Human trafficking is something that has been a hot topic for the last several years. I always had the image of trafficking from the movie *Taken*[3] where two young women go off to Europe by themselves, meet a good-looking guy, and then get abducted and sold into the sex trade. Lucky for one of them, Liam Neeson is her dad—okay, not really Liam Neeson, but you know—and he can kick some serious baduche (my made-up word for one's behind). That's action; that's Hollywood.

But the reality of what's happening in America is not Hollywood fiction, and it is happening in our own backyards every day. Human trafficking is not about kidnapping, abduction, or the horrors we see in movies and on social media. Don't get me wrong, it is horrific, but what we're seeing is much different from the movie Taken. What we are seeing is traffickers building false relationships and grooming our youth over a period of time, sometimes even a year or more. Further, there is a huge increase in familial trafficking, where family members are the traffickers. And to make it much easier for traffickers, social media and online gaming allow them to pursue our loved ones at the press of a button, so to speak. They are finding and luring our kids on and through social media and online gaming platforms.

I often hear misinformation surrounding human trafficking and what it looks like and doesn't look like. The majority of trafficked individuals are never kidnapped; they know their traffickers before they are ever trafficked. Further, the majority of trafficked individuals do not self-identify as being trafficked. There are numerous reasons for that, which we will explore later in this book, but these are all important distinctions to understand. So often, we, as parents and caregivers, may be looking for the white van to drive by and snatch up our kids. Although that is a terrifying thought, it doesn't happen very often. Again, traffickers specialize in building fake relationships with our children and young adults. That makes things a bit trickier for us as parents and caregivers, doesn't it? We should know who they are talking to both in the real world and online. That takes a tremendous amount of effort and time. But our kids are worth it.

So, what is human trafficking? Human trafficking involves the use of force, fraud, or coercion to compel another person to engage in labor or a commercial sex act.[4] Force, fraud, and coercion are keywords. Force, of course, is making someone do something against his or her will. And that is what we most often think about when we think about human trafficking: someone is being kidnapped and shipped overseas. Now, back to the movie Taken and Liam Neeson, or Bryan Mills and his "very particular set of skills."[5]

As a mom of two daughters and a son, I always thought that as long as I didn't send my daughters to Europe by themselves, we'd be good! And of course, if Liam Neeson were their dad, it wouldn't hurt either. I love my husband;

I've just never seen him take down three guys in a kitchen. But I digress. It suffices to say that the movie is a fantasy in a very creative writer's mind. And although that, in and of itself, is not a bad thing, it is definitely not what we see here in the Western world.

That leaves us with the key words fraud and coercion. Fraud is deception and lying, and coercion is manipulating someone through psychological force. If we were to tally the social media posts, movies, and news stories about trafficking, force would be the dominant action used in the force-fraud-coercion equation. This is why when we think of human trafficking, we associate it with kidnapping. It's sensational and exciting. It sells movies and draws people in.

However, if we look at the reality of human trafficking, force is the least likely tool used in the luring of individuals by traffickers. Fraud and coercion are much more predominant. Why in the world would that be? Here is how I often explain it to audiences: If I were to kidnap you and throw you in my white van, drug you, and sell you, would you be a good product for me? Probably not. You would be terrified, high on drugs, and want to fight back. That's simply not the best way to get someone to do what you want.

What if, instead, I became the mom you never had? What if I took care of you and filled your needs, I gave you a place to live, clothes to wear, and food to eat. More importantly, what if I met your emotional needs and made you feel loved, listened to, and cared for? Then, after a year of grooming you, I told you that we couldn't pay our rent. In order to help the family, I need you to have sex with someone for money, just one time, maybe two times, five times at the most. Now, are you going to be a good product for me? Absolutely!

But what changed? Trust. You trust and love me. And here is the most important thing: You think you chose this. That's how traffickers work. They take time, sometimes a lot of time–building a relationship and then using manipulation and coercion until they have that person doing exactly what they say.

So why do we miss it sometimes? Why do we have a misunderstanding when it comes to who is being trafficked? Let me give you an example. First, let's consider a young girl we'll call Maya. Maya is 12 years old, and one day she is on her way home from school in her middle-class neighborhood. All of a sudden, someone driving a creepy white van pulls up, jumps out to grab her, and kidnaps her. What do we do as a society? There's no question. We look for her! We may put up missing-person posters, air her story on the news, organize search parties, and diligently look for her.

Next, let's consider another young girl we'll call Mika. Mika is around the same age; however, she lives in a less affluent part of town. She's in a relationship with someone and falls in love. Mika comes from a bit of a troubled family, and this new relationship is not the best influence. Mika's new love convinces her that they should run away together, and so she leaves. Now what are we doing as a society? Are we putting missing posters out there? Do we see her story on the evening news? Are we sending out search parties? No, we are not.

In the case of Maya, who do we blame for her disappearance? We blame the kidnapper. And in Mika's situation, who do we blame? We blame Mika. And yet, in Mika's situation, it could be that she is the victim of a trafficker.

When you hear the word trafficking, you may think of something that happens far away, perhaps even in another country, or maybe you believe that such things only happen to other people. The reality is that human trafficking happens right here in the United States, in every single state. It affects people of all ages, races, and backgrounds—and yes, it affects kids.

A lot of confusion exists about what trafficking really is, so it's important to start with clear definitions.

Sex trafficking

With minors, sex trafficking happens when someone under the age of 18 (or 19 in some states) is exploited sexually in exchange for anything of value. It doesn't matter if the young person agreed, and it doesn't matter if there was no obvious violence. If anything of value is exchanged—money, food, a place to sleep, drugs, or even clothes or rides—it is always sex trafficking.

For adults, sex trafficking occurs when force, fraud, or coercion is used to compel someone into sexual acts in exchange for something of value. Again, that value can be money, but it can also be survival needs like shelter or food.

Sex trafficking can take many forms, such as pornography, child sexual abuse images (which we do not call child porn because minors cannot consent to pornography), exotic dancing, escorting, or what looks like prostitution. But almost no one in sex work is there by true choice.

Warning signs can include:

- Access to hotel keys, prepaid gift cards, or multiple cell phones.
- Sudden changes in appearance, such as new, expensive clothes or accessories.
- Talking about, or bragging about, having lots of money with no clear explanation.

Anyone can be trafficked for sex, including infants, children, teens, adults, and even senior citizens. It is shocking, and it should be. Because no matter the age, it is never okay for someone to be treated as a product and sold.

Labor trafficking

Labor trafficking is when force, fraud, or coercion is used to compel someone to work or provide services. In the United States, this often shows up in different types of service industries:

- Agriculture and farm labor
- Construction
- Domestic work, such as cleaning or childcare
- Restaurants (especially in back-of-house kitchens)

- Nail salons and massage parlors
- Landscaping and janitorial crews
- Traveling sales crews (selling magazines, candy, or trinkets)
- Food plants

In these situations, people may have their identification taken away, be charged impossible fees for job placements, or have food and housing tied to their performance. Often, they live in overcrowded, unsafe conditions, and they can't realistically leave.

Forced criminalization

Another form of labor trafficking is forced criminalization, which is when traffickers use control to force someone into criminal activity. This can include shoplifting, theft, begging, peddling, selling drugs or vapes, or transporting illegal goods. Victims may become hypervigilant around authorities because they know they are being forced to break laws.

Sometimes sex trafficking and labor trafficking overlap, and a person may be exploited for both at the same time. In either case, that person's dignity and value never change. Being trafficked does not make someone less than. People don't lose their worth because of what someone else does to them.

Labor exploitation vs. labor violations vs. labor trafficking

This can be confusing, so let's break it down:

- **Labor exploitation** is a broad term for unfair treatment in the workplace.
- **Labor violations** are actions that break employment laws.
- **Labor trafficking** is when force, fraud, or coercion are used to compel someone to work or provide services.

Not every unfair or illegal practice is trafficking, but sometimes the lines blur. And here's the key for parents and kids alike: You don't have to figure out what category it falls into. If something feels uncomfortable, is unsafe, or seems wrong, the right response is always to tell a trustworthy adult.

Why we talk about this

You might be wondering, *Why should I be learning about this as a parent?* The answer is simple: because trafficking is not just something that happens far away; it happens in every community. Your kids are hearing about it, whether from peers, online, or in the news. Talking about it at home prepares them.

And if your child ever witnesses something concerning or experiences grooming themselves, your open, informed conversations could be the reason he or she comes to you instead of staying silent.

People who are trafficked often don't report it. And why that may seem hard to believe, there are several reasons this may happen.

- They may not recognize it as trafficking.
- They may feel shame or embarrassment.
- They may believe it's their fault.
- The trafficker may be providing their basic needs like food or shelter, creating dependency.

By naming these realities and normalizing the conversation, you equip your child to recognize red flags and trust you as a safe place.

Often with human trafficking, we are looking for the wrong things. We're looking for the creepy white van driving by and taking our kids. We are not looking for the youth in a relationship that seems off.

That's why the foundation of human trafficking prevention must recognize that everyone has intrinsic value and that no one can change that fact.

Let's imagine that I had a $20 bill. If I held it up and asked you if you wanted it, my guess is you would say yes. What if I crumpled it up, stomped on it, and called it a disgusting, worthless $20 bill? Still yes? What if I coughed and sneezed on it? Would you still want it then?

I hope your answer is absolutely, yes! I hope you know that money is already dirty and hand sanitizer works. Of course you still want that $20 because its value has not changed, no matter what's been done with it or to it.

Our youth, and adults too, need to know that they have an intrinsic value that cannot be changed. It doesn't matter who they are or where they go. It doesn't matter how much money they have or don't have. It doesn't matter what their grades are. It doesn't matter how many followers they have on social media or how many likes their posts receive. None of those things matter because all youth have an intrinsic value that cannot be changed. And so do you.

This is critical to understand. And do you know what else is critical to understand? The same is true for every other person on this planet. Everyone else has an intrinsic value that cannot be changed.

The Set Me Free Project

How in the world did you get involved in the counter-trafficking movement?

That is a question I receive all the time. Let me tell you. I joined the movement kicking and screaming. As much as I believe it is a remarkably important fight—and it is—it was not a fight I wanted to join. I was comfortable with my head firmly planted in the sand. We often have our heads in the sand. Now, please don't get me wrong. I don't fault people for burying their heads in the sand. After all, mine was firmly planted. Let's face it. It's warm, comfy, and dark in there. And when we have our heads in the sand and don't look around, it's not because we are horrible people but because we simply aren't aware.

I was a mom of three kiddos, and thinking about the risk of human trafficking happening in the world, let alone in my own community, was absolutely horrifying. As a survivor of sexual and domestic violence and a recovering alcoholic, I had a desire to see women live healthy and successful lives. I worked with women and spoke all over the nation on topics specifically for women. Later, I added youth to the mix.

I loved it. I love speaking and making a difference in the lives of women and youth. I was happily running a nonprofit women's organization, writing curriculum, speaking to women all over the United States, and speaking to youth on the importance of healthy relationships.

It certainly was never my goal to run a counter-human trafficking organization. In fact, if you were to go back 20 years and ask me if I would be doing this, I would have said no way. And it's not that I don't care about people. Quite the opposite is true. It simply never occurred to me that this was a problem in our community.

Isn't that the way it is? So often we don't view something as a concern unless it has hit close to home. The minute I realized human trafficking was happening right around me, I had to do something. As William Wilberforce so famously stated, "You may choose to look the other way, but you can never again say you did not know."[6]

At that time, my children were attending

school in our state's biggest school district. I realized that if they had never learned they were at risk for human trafficking and I had never learned they were targets, we could not be atypical.

And then one day, my co-worker and soon-to-be co-founder said this: Let's help sex-trafficked victims. (That's an actual quote.) And having no idea what that meant, I agreed! So, teaming up with my co-founder, Cindy Hultine, we went to work. We began trying to determine what joining this fight would look like. We knew we weren't the right people to work one-on-one with trafficked individuals. That would only lead to more trauma for the survivor (no, seriously). And we certainly knew we weren't in the recovery business. Finally, after months and months of research and study, including talking to survivors, former traffickers, and many educators in the community, we decided that there was simply no education and prevention training on human trafficking.

When we, as individuals, recognize our intrinsic value, we see ourselves differently. When we, as individuals, value each other, we can only treat others with respect. We can't bully them, and we certainly can't sell or buy them. And so our curriculum was written with the foundation of telling our youth that they have value, because that's what they need to know. Frankly, that's what we need to know too.

As we continued our research, we began to look at other states, and although there was some prevention education on trafficking in larger communities, programs were few and far between. We were officially moved. Just like Mr. Wilberforce said, now that we knew, we had to do something.

In addition, when we found out that only 1–2% of trafficked individuals are identified and recovered, we deemed that unacceptable.[7] We determined to bring prevention education to communities across the Midwest and more, and our mission was born: to stop human trafficking before it starts by providing prevention education to all ages.

According to the International Labour Organization in 2024, human trafficking is a $236 billion industry.[8] Human trafficking results in trauma that impacts survivors, as well as their families, friends, and communities. Though every member of our community has the potential to be trafficked regardless of age, gender, or socioeconomic status, youth are especially vulnerable to the techniques used by traffickers. Because of this, we wanted to reach as many individuals as possible in order to build a more educated, equipped, and resilient city.

Although we started off with extremely humble beginnings, we now have a research-based curriculum with age-appropriate material for youth in kindergarten through college. The lessons begin with education on the importance of human dignity and value, social media safety, and consent, with the topic of human trafficking introduced in the seventh grade. Further, we educate adults in every facet of the community, including specific industries, because we all see human trafficking, even though we may not realize it. The READY to Stand Curriculum we developed is the product of years of experience in prevention education, detailed research, and feedback from experts in the human trafficking field, survivors, and researchers.

I think it's important to share that we are a bit unique in our curriculum and the way we present it. Despite the topic, which is a hard and scary topic, we think it's extremely important to empower and engage instead of terrifying people. And so we have a lot of fun. We laugh a lot with our presentation. And we say that although we take the topic very seriously, we don't take ourselves very seriously. Students of all ages can benefit from using humor to increase their retention because it stimulates the brain's dopamine reward system, leading to increased, goal-oriented motivation and long-term memory.[9]

So why prevention?

As I previously stated, and it's worth repeating, the percentage of identification, restoration, and recovery for people who have been trafficked is only 1% to 2%, making the prevention of human trafficking an absolute necessity. Those who can recover from trafficking (which is a lifelong recovery) go through a substantial amount of agony and anguish due to the scenario. When we work to prevent human trafficking in our communities, it helps prevent a great deal of suffering and anguish.

How many of you have seen the LifeLock commercial where a guy is sitting in the dentist chair ready to have what looks like an extremely uncomfortable procedure to repair a cavity? The dentist and the dental hygienist walk in, look at the guy's teeth, and announce that he has a bad cavity. In fact, they tell him it's not just bad, it's really bad, and then they begin to leave for lunch. The guy, reasonably concerned, asks through his mouth contraption if they were going to fix it. And that's when the dentist tells him, "I'm not a dentist. I'm a dental monitor." And the tagline? Why monitor a problem if you're not going to fix it?

I believe that awareness around the subject of human trafficking is a bit like that. People come in and tell you that human trafficking is bad, really bad even, and that's it, seemingly leaving us to ask: *Now what? What do we do?*

I have been honored to speak to youth and adults all over about the truth of human trafficking, sexual violence, social media safety, and healthy relationships. I have spoken and trained people who know a tremendous amount about human trafficking and to people who had no idea it even exists in the United States. And when I get the opportunity to speak, I always ask one question: Do you know your kids and grandkids are at risk?

This question often causes many in the room to look at me as if I have horns on top of my head. *What?! Not my kids! My kids are from a good family, living in a good neighborhood, with a good group of friends. My kids are at risk?* And my answer is always: *Yes, your kids are at risk for human trafficking.*

But if there are people hearing a message that human trafficking is not just bad but really bad, and yet, they don't recognize that their very own children and loved ones are at risk for this heinous crime, aren't we doing a disservice to those families in bringing awareness?

The answer is yes. I have had a lot of people tell me that everyone is out there teaching awareness. While it may be true that a lot of organizations and individuals are raising awareness, but prevention education is very different.

Prevention education is not just telling people that smoking is bad but showing people how to stop smoking or, even better, never start in the first place. Prevention education is not just saying it's important to wear a seatbelt but explaining why it is important and how to stay safe. Prevention education takes a problem and enables us to see that we could be affected and how we can prevent it from happening to us and our loved ones.

That's why we do what we do, to help youth and families see themselves in this problem of sex trafficking. We teach the truth that my kiddos and, yes, your kiddos are at risk of trafficking.

Now, here is the trick: Despite what people think, that message can't be founded in fear. Please don't get me wrong. Human trafficking is a terrifying topic, but in order to teach our kiddos about it, we don't need to make it more terrifying. It already is. We need to educate in a way that brings out critical thinking skills. That's exactly why the more questions we ask in a constructive way, as opposed to preaching on the topic, the better it will be received.

The sex work controversy

There is a controversy in our society about the viability of sex work as a profession. Some might refer to it as "the oldest profession" or "prostitution". The controversy is this: Women should be able to choose sex work as a profession to empower them to do what they want. Further, sex work should be legalized for the safety of sex workers and to minimize the abuse of sex trafficking.

Although I appreciate the sentiment, I approach it a bit differently. As a survivor of sexual and domestic violence, someone who experienced much objectification as a teen and a young adult, and someone who almost chose sex work as a young adult, I know that trauma can change the way we think. I understand the argument that legalization may increase safety and reduce harm, and I don't dismiss that perspective lightly. But I also believe we have to be honest about the full picture. Trauma, prior victimization, poverty, coercion, and manipulation can all shape what looks like choice from the outside. Agency and vulnerability are not opposites; they often live side by side. Sometimes a person is making a choice but choosing from options that were already narrowed by pain, survival, or circumstance.

My deeper concern is practical, not political: when exploitation can hide behind the appearance of consent, how do we reliably identify trafficking, coercion, or control? If many exploited individuals do not immediately recognize or identify themselves as trafficked, then separating voluntary participation from abuse becomes far more complicated than many public conversations admit. We owe people enough honesty to acknowledge that complexity.

I was asked to speak to a group of college students. The professor requested my expertise specifically to share that sex work was bad and change the minds of the students who were primarily pro sex work. I thought it was an interesting assignment and asked the professor what their knowledge of human trafficking was. She quickly explained that they were extremely knowledgeable when it came to human trafficking, and it wasn't necessary to discuss human trafficking, just the concern of sex work.

As I stood in front of the students, I immediately recognized that if they had no understanding or knowledge of human trafficking, I would not be able to aptly address sex work. I also quickly noticed that the conversation the professor was having with the students about the topic was a bit more telling than asking. In other words, she was simply letting them know they were wrong.

After I introduced myself, I urged the students to tell me what they knew about human trafficking. What was extremely interesting was that they really did not have a strong knowledge of human trafficking. So that's where we began: defining human trafficking, debunking a lot of myths, and discussing how the manipulation of a trafficker changes the mindset of an individual being trafficked.

Next, instead of saying what I believed about sex work, I asked questions—a lot of questions. If someone doesn't identify as being trafficked, could that person believe he or she was doing this by choice? If the trafficker has built a relationship with the individual being trafficked, how is that person supposed to know the trafficker is someone who wants to do harm? The more questions I asked, the more the students began to question their own beliefs about sex work being a viable profession. The more they began to understand the tricks and manipulation of a trafficker, the more they questioned choosing sex work as a profession. By the end of our time together, many of the students had a different viewpoint.

It's important to note that I am not saying that there are no people who have chosen sex work as their profession. However, I *am* saying that often when someone believes he or she has chosen sex work, it may not truly be a choice because of fraud and coercion. It may also be true that a different choice would have been made without the influence of trauma.

Why do I tell that story? Because it is critical that we are careful and intentional about how we talk to our youth about these subjects. Telling them "don't do this" and "don't do that" will only pique their interest and might move them toward the very thing we want them to avoid. Instead, it's about critical thinking. Our youth are smart, brilliant even, and they can make solid decisions when guided in the right direction.

***

Take-home tip: Human trafficking doesn't always look like abduction. Often it looks like a trusted relationship being misused. Keep open conversations going at home. Kids who feel safe talking with you are harder for traffickers to manipulate.

CHAPTER 2

My kids? Really?

One of the things I hear often is that people think human trafficking can't possibly happen in their communities, or at least it can't happen to their kids. Unfortunately, those words could not be more false. All of our youth are at risk, regardless of the family they live with, the amount of money they have or don't have, or the friends they keep. Traffickers go after the vulnerable, and we are all vulnerable at any given time. And although there are people who have multiple vulnerabilities, it's important to recognize that youth of all backgrounds are at risk for human trafficking.

There are a lot of misconceptions that travel around about human trafficking. In fact, the misconceptions may even come from organizations that should know better. Let's go over a few of these misconceptions and discuss why they are wrong and how they can cause harm.

When we are looking for the wrong thing, it's easier to miss what really is happening, which is why we must dispel the myths and the hype around human trafficking. When we believe stereotypes and falsities, we create a false narrative of what human trafficking is. We also risk missing the things we need to see in order to understand what it is and what it isn't.

Myth 1: Males are rarely trafficked.

It is extremely common that when we hear about human trafficking, specifically sex trafficking, we hear about a young blonde-haired, blue-eyed girl, particularly in the United States. The truth is, however, that males are often trafficked for both sex and labor. It is simply a myth that only women and girls are trafficked.[10]

But if that's the case, why do we only hear about cases involving women and girls? Human trafficking is a crime that brings layers upon layers of trauma upon those victimized, and this is true for all who are trafficked. However, society has created a safer space for females to disclose. Although there is often a tremendous amount of shame surrounding the disclosure for any individual, we have set males up for failure.

Males grow up hearing phrases such as, "Man up," "Suck it up, buttercup," or the classic, "Boys don't cry." We have formed a society where males are often too ashamed to disclose, or they may not even recognize that they can be victimized in such a way. But the truth is that in some areas males are trafficked for sex almost as often as females.

At The Set Me Free Project, we don't work with survivors directly or do direct service. Still, we receive a lot of calls from people trying to flee a trafficking situation, survivors needing help, or family members dealing with a child who is being trafficked. One afternoon, I was working when a distraught mother called me in tears. She relayed that her son was caught in a trafficking situation while gaming with someone he thought was a friend. He wound up being trafficked by a group of young men in his own community, and his mom was looking for help.

We hear similar stories quite often. To assume that only a certain gender, race, culture, or (fill in the blank) is being trafficked is a good way to miss what is really happening in our communities.

Myth 2: Trafficked individuals are desperate to escape and will ask for help when they need it.

Because human trafficking is about building relationships (albeit fake ones) and not kidnapping, most trafficked individuals are bonded to their traffickers. Traffickers are most often someone they know; that could be a romantic partner, a family member, or someone they may consider a friend.

How is it possible that someone cannot see an individual as a threat when they actually are? Why don't people leave abusive and destructive relationships? One of the reasons is a phenomenon called a trauma bond. According to *Psychology Today,* a trauma bond is an emotional attachment that can develop in an abusive relationship, specifically between the person suffering and the perpetrator of the abuse. A trauma bond is defined by cycles of negative reinforcement punctuated by brief bursts of positive reward. This so-called intermittent reinforcement makes it extremely difficult to exit an abusive relationship.[11]

Trafficked individuals often see the trafficker as someone who takes care of their needs, loves them, and is on their side. And the truth is, in a sick and harmful way, the trafficker *is* taking care of their needs. In fact, a survivor once said that if you want to help a trafficked individual, you had better be prepared to provide everything that the trafficker is providing and more.

Trafficked individuals are often not desperate because they believe they are at home with this individual. Keep in mind that familial trafficking, where a family member is doing the trafficking, is a huge issue not only globally but right here in the United States.

Myth 3: Human trafficking requires transporting.

This is a common myth that I often hear included when defining trafficking. It might go a bit like this: Human trafficking is taking someone against his or her will and transporting the individual somewhere. Although this is a story that is often told in the media, it isn't accurate. An individual who never leaves their home of origin can still be trafficked.

There was a young woman who was going to high school every day, getting straight A's, living with her parents, and being trafficked by her boyfriend every night. Mom and Dad were none the wiser.

As we mentioned earlier, familial trafficking is also a very common thing we see. In these cases, the traffickers are moms and dads, grandmas and grandpas, or aunts and uncles (and, of course, it's not limited to these family members). When this happens, transporting doesn't have to take place, as much of the trafficking happens near home.

When we are talking about labor trafficking, what we consider trafficking may look extremely different from our idea of sex trafficking. More on that later.

Myth 4: Most recruiting happens at gas stations or truck stops along major highways or interstates.

How many of you have heard the horror stories of truck stops and gas stations being the trafficking hubs of the United States? The truth is that although there are people trafficked (or sold) at truck stops, this is not the only place such things happen, and it definitely isn't where the majority of people are recruited. The key word here is *recruited*.

When I am training, I often share the story of something I witnessed that I still can't believe. If any of you have the Nextdoor app, you know that it's what I call comedy gold. People say some of the silliest things, and the comment section is filled with mean and, frankly, not very neighborly advice. One day, I was looking at the posts when someone posted that her daughter was sitting and reading a book in the middle of a roundabout in a neighborhood, often considered to be middle to upper class. She then shared that a black SUV drove by, stopped next to her daughter, and asked her if she wanted a ride home. The daughter said no, and after going back and forth several times, the daughter finally left the roundabout with a final *no*. As the SUV pulled away, she heard the people in the vehicle say, "Darn it." The poster's warning was to be careful out there and protect your children.

This is where the advice and comments began quickly. One woman posted that she was not surprised because human trafficking is at an all-time high. The second comment was from a woman who simply said, "That wasn't human trafficking." This statement intrigued commenter number one who asked if it wasn't human trafficking, then what was it.

Commenter number two, who I will now refer to as CN2, relayed that she knew it wasn't human trafficking because she was trained at work, and human trafficking doesn't happen in that small town. Now, I have to admit, I am more of a stalker on social media than I am a commenter, but when I see a comment about human trafficking that is riddled in misconceptions, I have to say something. And so, I posted that yes, CN2 was probably correct in that it wasn't human trafficking. But then I added that trafficking definitely does happen in that small town and, in fact, it is happening everywhere. Well, that began a bit of a comment war, in which CN2 reminded me that she was trained at work and knows that human trafficking can't happen in that small town because—wait for it—that small town has roundabouts. Roundabouts! And CN2 let us know that you can't get trafficked in a town that has roundabouts.

Of course, this is absolutely ridiculous. In fact, it's one of the most ridiculous things I have ever heard. Her final point was that a trafficker needs an interstate or a highway for a quick getaway, and if a town has a roundabout, that is simply not possible. It didn't take long for me to explain that trafficking is often a relationship-building crime, and neither kidnapping nor a fast getaway is necessary for a trafficker.

These are the misconceptions that can be out there. The myths shared are not the only myths out there, but they are certainly a few.

The grooming process

In my work with education and prevention, especially regarding human trafficking, we talk about the grooming process quite a bit. It's something that has a profound impact on an individual. And here's the thing: The grooming process doesn't just happen in situations of sexual violence. It can happen in violent romantic relationships as well, and sometimes the person doing the grooming may not even fully realize what he or she is doing. It might be intentional, but it might not. Regardless, it's still a part of the manipulation process.

The grooming process is something we focus on a lot when we talk about human trafficking prevention. It's not a sudden or obvious thing; it's a gradual process that traffickers use to gain control over someone.

And here's the hard truth: the person who goes into the grooming process is never the same person who comes out. It changes the person, and that's what makes it so dangerous.

When we think about human trafficking, we often imagine force or kidnapping, but the reality is that most traffickers use manipulation and grooming to get what they want. Grooming is about building trust and creating dependency, and it doesn't always look sinister at first. In fact, it can seem like a normal or even caring relationship in the beginning.

It starts with the trafficker targeting someone, often someone with vulnerabilities. Maybe the person is struggling emotionally, socially, or financially. These aren't weaknesses, but they are openings a trafficker can exploit. The trafficker gains the person's trust, and that can look like kindness, shared interests, or even romance. The trafficker makes the person feel special, understood, and/or loved. For someone who's craving that validation or connection, it feels like he or she has found someone who truly cares. But that's just the beginning.

After they gain your trust, the trafficker starts to fill a need. That could be emotional support, financial help, or a sense of belonging. For many victims, they're getting something they feel they've been missing in their lives, and they don't even realize they're being manipulated. The trafficker then begins to isolate them, slowly pulling them away from friends, family, and any other support system. "Your family doesn't really care about you," they might say, or "I'm the only one who truly understands you." It's all about making the person dependent on the trafficker.

Once that control has been gained, the exploitation begins. This is where trafficking happens—whether it's forced labor, commercial sex, or another form of exploitation. By this point, the victim may feel so trapped and disconnected that he or she doesn't even see a way out. The trafficker maintains control, using fear, manipulation, or threats to keep the person under control.

Educating ourselves and others about how this process works is one of the most powerful ways we can stop human trafficking before it starts.

So, how does grooming work? It starts with targeting. They identify someone who has a vulnerability, something they can exploit. Then, they gain trust. This part can feel wonderful. They'll do things like say, "Oh my gosh, you love dogs? I love dogs too! We have so much in common!" It feels so natural and amazing at first, and the target may feel truly understood.

After that, they fill a need. This might look like compliments or affection, things that make the target feel valuable or special. For me personally, I craved validation that I felt I didn't get from my biological father. I needed to feel worth, value, and love, and when I was young, I didn't understand that my worth was intrinsic and didn't depend on anyone else. But when you're in that vulnerable state, you think those things have to come from someone else.

Then, after they've gained trust and filled a need, the next step is isolation. They slowly start cutting the target off from any support system. After that comes exploitation, which could be sexual or otherwise. Finally, they maintain control. If they've done the first three steps well, those last three become a lot easier to pull off.

What's important to remember is that once people have gone through the grooming process, they're never the same. It fundamentally changes them, and that's why it's so critical for us to be aware of the signs and to help others recognize what's happening before it gets to that point.

Vulnerabilities

Traffickers are incredibly skilled at identifying vulnerabilities, and the truth is that every single one of us has them. It's important to recognize that these vulnerabilities aren't necessarily weaknesses, but they are aspects of our lives that traffickers can exploit in their pursuit of control. Vulnerabilities can manifest in various forms, whether it's something as common as being active on social media or gaming platforms or something more deep-rooted like experiencing feelings of loneliness or lacking a strong support system.

Mental health challenges, physical disabilities, financial struggles, and even a basic human need for connection are all things that traffickers look for. Once a trafficker identifies these vulnerabilities, the next move is to gain the individual's trust. This can happen quickly because traffickers are experts at recognizing what a person is missing in life and then swoop in to fill that void. It might be through offering money, providing friendship, showing love, or creating a false sense of security and support.

One of the most powerful tools traffickers use is targeting emotional needs. They understand just how deeply we all crave connection, acceptance, and validation. By meeting these needs, they create a bond that can be very difficult to break. And it's not just about offering something tangible; traffickers know how to manipulate emotions, creating a dependency that can be as compelling as any physical trap. This is where their power lies in making someone feel seen, cared for, and valued, even when it's a manipulation to exploit that very trust.

So although traffickers go after the vulnerable, we all have vulnerabilities and any one of us could be at risk from someone who might want to do harm. There is no prerequisite that a vulnerable individual has to come from a troubled family life, be addicted to drugs, or somehow be whatever society deems "not good." It is all kiddos—yours and mine—who are at risk for human trafficking, and it is often in our homes because of social media.

One of the most important things to understand about human trafficking is this: Traffickers are not just looking for a specific type of person. They're looking for *opportunities*. They are skilled at spotting vulnerabilities, those moments in someone's life when physical, emotional, or relational needs are unmet, and then manipulating those vulnerabilities to gain control.

And here's what I want you to hear clearly: Having vulnerabilities does not make anyone less than or weak. Every single one of us has vulnerabilities at different points in our lives. That's part of being human. What matters is recognizing them and strengthening protective influences around our kids so that those vulnerabilities don't become entry points for people who want to do harm.

A vulnerability is anything that increases a person's risk of harm. It's not who your child is; it's something he or she experiences. And because of their circumstances, some children may face multiple vulnerabilities at once.

For example, youth in foster care or the juvenile justice system often carry added vulnerabilities. So do kids who face mental health challenges, poverty, or housing instability. But vulnerabilities can also be as common as feeling isolated at school, struggling with body image, or wanting the newest phone or gaming system.

Common vulnerabilities and how traffickers exploit them

Addiction: Traffickers may provide drugs or alcohol to keep someone dependent or use blackmail around things done while under the influence.

Housing insecurity: A trafficker might offer what they claim is a safe place to stay in exchange for sex or labor.

Poverty: Offering expensive clothes, shoes, or electronics can quickly turn into, "Now you owe me."

Abuse or neglect: Traffickers often play the role of rescuer, offering love, attention, or even meals—only to twist those needs into manipulation later.

Foster care or justice system involvement: These youth may already long for stability or belonging, which traffickers exploit.

Mental health struggles: Depression, anxiety, or trauma symptoms can make someone more vulnerable to promises of relief, attention, or escape.

Social media and gaming: Traffickers create online relationships, feeding unmet needs for attention, belonging, or validation, and then they exploit them.

Feeling *othered*: Kids who feel excluded or discriminated against may latch onto anyone who makes them feel seen and valued, even if that person is unsafe.

LGBTQ+ Youth: Youth who identify as LGBTQ+ can face increased vulnerability to human trafficking and exploitation, not because of their identity necessarily, but because they may experience family rejection, housing instability, isolation, or a lack of support systems.

Language barriers or immigration status: Limited communication or fear of deportation can be powerful tools traffickers use to trap someone.

What this means for parents/caregivers

- Having vulnerabilities does *not* mean your child will be trafficked.
- Vulnerabilities cannot always be fixed. Your child can't change his or her age, for example.
- What *can* make the difference is building strong, safe, loving relationships.

Traffickers are experts at building relationships that look real but are deeply manipulative. The best prevention we have is to build even stronger ones, authentic, trusting connections at home and in the community.

Traffickers thrive on isolation. They create networks of control. Parents and caregivers can push back by creating networks of support. When kids feel connected, valued, and loved, it is much harder for a trafficker to find a way in.

And one more reminder: Vulnerabilities do not change intrinsic value. No matter what your child faces, he or she is born with unchangeable worth. Nothing a trafficker does, and no circumstance a child experiences, can take that away.

Protective factors

After talking about vulnerabilities, it's just as important to shift the conversation toward protective influences, the people, skills, and resources that help keep kids safe and resilient. Traffickers are masters at spotting needs and weaknesses, but protective factors can act like anchors. They don't eliminate risk completely, but they provide stability and strength when life gets hard. Protective influences are those resources and relationships that reduce the risk of harm. Some are internal things within us, like resilience, faith, problem-solving, or self-awareness. Others are external things around us, like supportive adults, safe friendships, or a positive school environment.

As parents and caregivers, one of the most valuable roles we play is helping our children identify these protective influences in their own lives and cultivating the ones that are missing.

It's important to remember that just because a young person has vulnerabilities, it doesn't mean they are destined to be trafficked. And just because someone has protective factors, it doesn't mean trafficking could never happen to that person. The responsibility for trafficking always lies with the trafficker.

Still, when kids have strong protective factors, they are better equipped to recognize red flags, seek help, and resist manipulation. You can help by:

- Encouraging safe, trustworthy relationships with mentors, teachers, coaches, or extended family.
- Modeling healthy coping strategies for stress, like journaling, prayer, exercise, or talking openly about feelings.
- Supporting positive involvement in school, faith communities, or activities that build belonging.
- Reinforcing their intrinsic value: "You are not your struggles. You have unshakable worth."

What if my child doesn't see protective factors?

Some kids may feel like they don't have protective factors—or don't recognize them in their lives. That doesn't mean they're helpless. You can help them begin to develop protective influences by:

- Talking about their strengths ("You're really good at noticing when something feels off. That's an important protective skill.")

- Helping them connect with safe adults and supportive communities.
- Encouraging growth in areas like self-awareness, resilience, or faith practices that bring comfort and perspective.

If your child has protective factors and still experiences harm, it is never the child's fault. Traffickers are expert manipulators, and even the strongest can be targeted. Protective influences don't guarantee safety, but they give kids tools they can reach for when life feels overwhelming.

At the heart of all of this is a truth that every child needs to hear over and over: "You are not defined by your vulnerabilities. You are more than your struggles, and nothing changes your intrinsic value."

Consent

Consent should be a foundational practice, and it's especially important to begin teaching it in schools from a young age. It's about instilling in children the knowledge that they are in control of their own bodies, and they alone get to decide who touches them and when. This lesson is critical in empowering young people to understand personal boundaries and bodily autonomy.

For example, I've always been a person who loves giving hugs. But even when it's with someone I know well, I always ask for consent. It's important to me that no one feels uncomfortable or obligated. My son, who's now an adult, was a big hugger when he was younger. But when he hit 13, he started pulling back from hugs. As much as it tugged at my heart, I understood that respecting his boundaries was crucial. Forcing a hug, even out of love, would send the wrong message—that he didn't have control over who touched him. And that's the last thing I wanted to communicate. It's all about empowering people to understand they have the right to make decisions about their own bodies.

I once worked with a survivor who said something that stuck with me: "A yes is not a yes if no is not an option." This statement is so powerful because it highlights that true consent requires the freedom to say no. Even something seemingly innocent, like placing a hand on a student's shoulder, can be triggering for someone who has experienced sexual abuse or trauma. In settings like medical care or caregiving, asking for consent is essential: "I'm about to touch your shoulder. Is that okay?" This simple question honors a person's autonomy. By modeling these behaviors, we foster respect and help others understand the importance of boundaries and personal choice.

Teaching and practicing consent is more than a courtesy; it's a lesson in respect, personal power, and dignity. The earlier we integrate these practices, the stronger the message that everyone deserves the right to decide what happens with his or her own body.

***

Take-home tip: Vulnerabilities don't define your child – they're simply areas that need extra care. Focus on building strong, safe relationships and networks because traffickers exploit isolation while resilience grows in connection.

Take-home tip: You don't need to eliminate every risk to protect your child. What matters most is building a web of safe people, healthy activities, and coping skills so your child has strong anchors when life gets tough.

CHAPTER 3

Social media and gaming

Let's face it. We are in a different day and age. When I was a kid, in order to connect with someone who was not right in front of me, I had to either write a letter or talk to someone on a corded phone attached to a wall. Yes, times are different. Today, we have access to the entire world at our fingertips. And when we have access to the world, the world has access to us. And so do our kids.

In this digital age, the online world offers opportunities that many of us couldn't imagine when we were young, and as a result, it also offers many hidden challenges. It is important to remember, however, that as caregivers, we can't wag our fingers and simply tell our youth to stay off social media. That won't do any good at all. Social media and online abilities are not going away. Instead, it is our job to help our youth safely navigate social media. In fact, it is important that they learn how to manage it while they are still in our homes. Helping them by having honest dialogues and setting safe boundaries will help them and you navigate this ever-changing world.

The landscape of social media

Let me tell you a couple of things that I feel strongly about. First of all, it's absolutely true that when our kids have access to the world through social media, the world also has access to them. That can be scary. But let me ask you this: Where is the best place to teach your child how to safely navigate social media? It's in your home.

I often hear parents say, "My kids aren't getting on social media until they're in high school." But I would take a different approach. I understand the reasoning—there are risks on social media, so the instinct is to keep them off it. That seems logical, right? But here's the reality: They will access social media at some point, likely somewhere outside of your control.

I'll never forget one experience I had with my son when he was just four years old. He's an adult now, but back then, we used to sit and watch YouTube together. We loved the Berenstain Bears—wholesome, classic fun. He didn't have his own tablet or device, so we always watched it together. Then one day, after several episodes had already played, a highly inappropriate, sexualized version of the Berenstain Bears came up. It was shocking. Someone had twisted those innocent cartoons into something deeply disturbing. That was a turning point for me.

Another time, my son came home, stood behind me, and casually dropped the f-bomb. He was only four years old! He knew it wasn't something he was supposed to say; I could see it on his face. We had a conversation, of course. He didn't hear that language in our home, and while it might've come from a relative's house, it's just as likely he picked it up elsewhere, maybe online.

Here's the thing: these are our kids, and this is the reality of what they're up against. But before we dive too deep, I don't want you walking away from this feeling scared; I want you to feel empowered. That's really the goal here. You have the tools right in front of you to help your kids navigate the digital world safely.

Here's something wild: When teens see a photo with tons of likes, their brains light up the same way ours do when we reconnect with an old friend or win an exciting prize. It's a massive reaction! And while we can't just hand them social media and smartphones without any guidance (because those dopamine hits are seriously powerful), we can teach them how to move through these spaces safely.

When I am speaking to parents, I always request a show of hands and ask how many of them would say that their children suffer from anxiety or depression. Often, when I ask this question during a webinar and parents can respond anonymously, those with youth in middle and high school are quick to raise their hands. It is typically quite a large percentage. And let me add that I am one of those parents. My kids have faced it too.

What I've found is that parents of older teens are more likely to acknowledge it, while parents of younger kids might not see it yet. But that doesn't mean it's not there; it often just takes a while to show up. And you know what plays a big role in that? Social media.

Think about it, how many of us have scrolled through Facebook, looked at someone's life, and thought, "Wow, she's got it all together. Look at those flowers her husband gets her. Their kids probably never argue." And then—*boom*—we feel lousy about our own situation. If that happens to us as adults, imagine how much more intense it is for teens. They're not just looking at these picture-perfect lives. They're editing their own photos, tweaking how they look, and even altering videos to fit an idealized version of themselves.

I once heard about a girl who had a mole on her face. In person, it was there, no big deal, but in every photo she posted, that mole was gone. She edited it out every single time. There is a constant pressure to look flawless, and it's exhausting. This is the kind of stuff our kids are dealing with, and it's impacting their brains in ways we can't always see.

Yes, the pressure from social media is real, and yes, it's tough. But this is where we come in. As parents, we need to model what healthy boundaries with technology look like.

So here's the thing: Your kids are probably getting exposed to social media somewhere, even if it's not through a phone or tablet in your home. All they need is a burner phone or access to someone else's device. That's why I always recommend introducing social media to them around seventh or eighth grade. It's not the enemy, even though at times it might feel that way. It's also important to recognize that it's not going anywhere any time soon. There is a high chance that our kids will eventually use it in their professional lives, so we want to equip them to navigate it safely, just like teaching them to drive. A car is dangerous if used recklessly, but we don't keep our kids from learning to drive because of that danger. The same goes for social media.

Now, let's talk about gaming for a second, because it's just as important. In fact, traffickers are increasingly using online gaming platforms to lure victims, even more so than through social media in some cases. It's a serious issue that needs attention.

Before I move on, I can almost feel the worried feelings, and I understand. But I want to stress that social media can be a positive tool if we help our kids learn to use it wisely. What I'm not advocating for is giving them unrestricted access. I'm not suggesting they have phones in their rooms or unsupervised time online. We need to set boundaries, of course.

Let me leave you with some statistics. Even though they're from a while ago, they're still relevant. One in six teens online has been contacted by someone who made them feel uncomfortable. One in three has received inappropriate advertising.[12] So we need to have conversations with our kids: what will they do if they see something that makes them feel uncomfortable? How will they respond?

Any guesses on the average age a boy first sees pornography? As of this writing, it's about 13 years old, with the youngest at about 5 years old. And for girls, it's about 14 years old when they first see pornography.[13]

Although it is very challenging to find true numbers, we know that the average age a girl is first trafficked is between approximately twelve and nineteen. For boys, it's not much different; in fact, it's often younger.[14]

We can see how important it is to teach our kids how to navigate this digital world safely. After all, they're going to be part of it, whether we like it or not.

I know it might sound like I'm talking out of both sides of my mouth right now, but bear with me, I'm going to tie it all together. Yes, the barrage of information and pressure from social media is real. Yes, it's tough. But this is where we come in. We need to model what healthy boundaries with technology look like.

Our kids should have the chance to experience social media under our supervision, in our homes, where we can guide them. And we need to model that same balance ourselves. If we're on our phones at dinner, we're sending a message that's hard to take back. One of the best pieces of advice I ever received as a parent was this: When your child walks into the room, let your face light up like they're the most amazing thing you've ever seen. It's a simple but powerful gesture.

I was at the orthodontist with my daughter one day, and we were waiting when I noticed a dad and his little girl. She must have been around nine, and she was twirling around, trying to get her dad's attention. He was glued to his phone the whole time. No matter how many spins she did, she couldn't get him to look up. That broke my heart. We have to model for our kids that they are more important than our phones.

Now, for those of you with elementary-aged kids, I don't recommend giving them social media just yet. But I do recommend having conversations about it. I guarantee they know what TikTok and Snapchat are. Start asking questions: "Do your friends have phones? What do they say about TikTok? What do you know about Snapchat?" Then, as they get older, in middle school or high school, you can slowly introduce social media in a safe and controlled way.

When you give them access, make it clear: This is my phone. Remember, you own it, and you can take it at any time. Some parents tell me, "If my kid gets in trouble with social media, I'll just take the phone away." But that's not always the answer, because it's easy for them to access someone else's phone and get back online. All they need is Wi-Fi, and they can access any social media they want.

Once they're on social media, monitor it closely. Follow them, have their passwords—not just to their phone but to every account. Kids can be fast when it comes to hiding things. They might have a finsta (fake Instagram) or secret accounts on other platforms. I'll show you how to find some of those later, but for now, just know that monitoring is crucial.

And don't forget, it's not just about social media, it's about all their devices. When it's time to check their phones, grab everything: phone, tablet, laptop, watch, whatever they have. Go through the browser history, messages, apps, and even scroll through all their app pages to see what they're hiding. Yes, it's time-consuming, but it's worth it.

As parents, we need to be approachable at all times. And to do that, you can't immediately react when your kid brings something to you that makes your hair curl—trust me, I know how hard that can be. When your child comes to you and says, "I need to talk to you," or if you find something on his or her phone, your first instinct might be to freak out. I'll never forget the first time I saw my oldest daughter's social media. I was absolutely appalled. I thought, *This is not how we raised her! What is going on here?*

But if your reaction is to snap, "I cannot believe you're posting this!" what's going to happen? They're going to shut down. They won't come to you again, and that's the last thing you want. The first time I found my daughter's secret Instagram account (her finsta), we were in the car, just her and me, heading somewhere fun. I said, "Oh, by the way, I found your finsta." I could sense the panic in her. I calmly said, "You've got two choices: Either you let me follow you, or you delete it. Totally up to you." And you know what? She deleted it.

It's so important to have open conversations with our teens if we want to build strong, trusting relationships with them. When we make ourselves approachable and create a space where they feel comfortable sharing their thoughts and feelings, we're building the foundation for trust. And trust is the key to any healthy relationship. Teens are naturally seeking independence. They're figuring out who they are, but they still need guidance. When they trust us, they're more likely to come to us with their concerns rather than keeping them bottled up or turning to less reliable sources.

By maintaining open lines of communication, we're also in a better position to offer advice and influence their decisions in a way that doesn't feel overbearing or judgmental.

This guidance is crucial as they navigate difficult situations like peer pressure, online dangers, or challenges with mental health. If we've fostered an open dialogue, they'll know they can turn to us before those problems spiral out of control.

Talking openly also plays a big role in their emotional health. When teens feel heard, they know that their feelings are valid, and this sense of validation is so important for developing emotional resilience. They need to know that even when life gets messy, we're here to listen, not to judge.

Moreover, teens who feel they can talk to their parents are less likely to engage in risky behavior. If they feel comfortable coming to us about tough topics, whether it's peer pressure to drink or experiment with drugs or issues like unhealthy relationships, we can intervene and guide them before things escalate. And when we consistently communicate in a supportive way, we help them build self-esteem. When they believe their voices are valued, their confidence grows, which, in turn, helps them make better decisions and stand up for themselves in difficult situations.

It's also about preparing them for life. Open communication gives us a chance to step back and allow them to express their views, make mistakes, and learn from those mistakes, all while knowing we're there for support. This helps them build critical thinking skills and fosters independence, which is exactly what they need to navigate adulthood successfully.

Ultimately, keeping that dialogue going strengthens our connection. It's not just about guiding them through challenges; it's about building a deeper bond and reinforcing the idea that no matter what, we're here for them. When we have those honest, meaningful conversations, we create shared experiences that foster mutual respect and understanding.

This not only benefits them but brings us closer as a family.

The digital world our kids navigate every day is anything but simple. As parents and caregivers, it's important for us to understand not just the incredible opportunities these platforms provide but also the real dangers that exist on Instagram, Snapchat, TikTok, and beyond.

Social media has woven itself into the fabric of our kids' lives, shaping how they see themselves and how they connect with the world. This book is all about helping you, as a parent or caregiver, keep them safe while they engage with these platforms. We're going to walk through the steps to open up important conversations, set healthy boundaries, and recognize the potential risks they face online.

Before we can really protect and guide our kids, we need to understand the spaces they're hanging out in online. Every platform has its own culture and language, not to mention its own set of risks. Whether it's the quick, fleeting posts on Snapchat or the endless, viral videos on TikTok, these platforms are captivating our kids. And as parents, it's up to us to know where our kids are—both physically and in the cyber world. This chapter will break down today's social media landscape so you can feel more confident guiding your child and keeping them safe.

One of the best ways to keep our kids safe online is by creating a space where they feel comfortable talking about their experiences. In this chapter, we'll explore how to have meaningful, judgment-free conversations about social media with your children. It's about asking the kinds of questions that invite them to share, not shut down. The goal is to build a partnership, not a policing operation. When our kids feel safe coming to us, we can spot potential red flags together and early on.

Setting boundaries isn't always easy, especially when you're trying to raise a confident, independent human in a digital world that moves faster than we do. But boundaries matter. They are not about control; they are about care. As your child grows, the goal is to balance their expanding independence with the wisdom and protection they still need. Healthy social media guidelines create safety without shame and structure without fear. When you invite your child into the conversation, listening, explaining, and collaborating, boundaries become less about restriction and more about trust. And trust is what truly keeps kids safer online.

Cyberbullying, privacy concerns, inappropriate content, and yes, even human trafficking, are real risks in today's digital world. But we don't respond with panic; we respond with awareness and preparation. When we understand what's out there, we can have calm, confident conversations with our kids about it. The goal isn't to scare them, it's to equip them. By building resilience, strengthening critical thinking, and keeping communication open, we help our children learn how to navigate challenges instead of being overwhelmed by them. Protection matters, but empowerment lasts.

No one's perfect, and mistakes are going to happen. Whether it's oversharing on social media, talking to the wrong people, or just spending too much time glued to the screen, your child will probably slip up. This is about how we, as parents, can take those inevitable missteps and turn them into meaningful moments of growth. Instead of reacting with shame or fear, we choose curiosity, conversation, and connection, helping our kids learn, adjust, and move forward stronger and wiser than before. By creating a home environment where children feel supported, not judged, we can help them learn from their digital missteps and grow in responsibility.

At the heart of everything we do as parents is the relationship we have with our kids. Our goal is to walk through their digital journey with them, offering guidance, empathy, and unwavering support. By using the tools in this book, we can build stronger relationships with our children, ensuring they not only navigate social media safely but also learn to use it wisely. At the end of the day, it's all about trust, understanding, and keeping the conversation going.

But what do I need to know about social media?

Let's get real for a minute, this digital world we're living in? It's incredible. Social media and gaming can be fun, creative, and even a great way for kids to stay connected. But we have to teach our kids how to navigate it safely because traffickers are using these same platforms to build relationships and groom their next target.

Yes, I will repeat it again because we must understand this. Trafficking is not about kidnapping; it's about connection. And two of the most common places traffickers build that connection are social media and online games.

We may not think twice about what we post, but traffickers are watching. And when a young person posts something vulnerable like, "I hate my life," or, "No one understands me," a trafficker can swoop in and respond, "I feel that way too. You can talk to me." Boom. Relationship started.

Traffickers are strategic. They're not lurking in the shadows waiting to kidnap someone—they're online, watching, and waiting for the right opportunity. And social media is their playground. It's one of the top places traffickers lure individuals.

This isn't about abductions. It's about building relationships, and social media makes that incredibly easy. It rarely starts with something dramatic. It starts with a post. A mood. A frustrated comment. A "no one gets me" kind of day. And then someone shows up, not loud, not creepy, not obvious. Just... understanding. "I get it." "You deserve better." "I'd never treat you that way."

That kind of validation feels good, especially to a teen who feels unseen or misunderstood. But sometimes that "safe" voice is strategic. People who exploit youth are incredibly patient. They watch for emotional cracks, step in with empathy, and slowly position themselves as the one person who truly understands. It doesn't begin with danger. It begins with connection.

It's subtle. It's sneaky. And it's strategic. That's why it's so important to talk to our kids about what they're posting, and who's watching. I always say, if you wouldn't stand in the middle of your town's busiest street shouting your personal business through a megaphone, don't do it online. But that's exactly what's happening. And while most people scroll right by, traffickers don't. They see an opportunity.

So what can you do? Start the conversation with your children. Not in a fear-based way, but in a *real* way. Ask your kids, "Would you want a complete stranger to know this about you?" Help them understand that privacy doesn't mean shame; it means protection.

And then keep talking. Keep asking. Stay engaged. Keep learning.

You don't need to know every detail about social media to keep your children safe.

What about gaming?

It's easy to understand why social media can be a scary place, but what about online gaming?

I hear it all the time: "But it's just a game." I get it. Gaming is fun, interactive, and, honestly, a big part of many kids' lives. But traffickers know that too, and they use it.

Here's what can happen: A trafficker will game with a young person for weeks, even months. They build rapport. They become "friends." Then the subtle questions start. "Is it snowing where you are?" "What time is it there?" Now they're gathering location info.

Next thing you know, they're chatting outside the game. Then they're asking to meet. It happens slowly, but it happens *all the time.*

I've heard story after story, gaming relationships that felt totally normal until, one day, they weren't.

So what can you do as a parent?

- Encourage your kids to game with people they actually know in the real world.
- If strangers join, don't use the mic. Don't chat.
- Remind them that anything said in your house (yes, including "Pick up your underwear!") can be heard by everyone in that game.

And this is important: Don't come in swinging with, "Delete all your games!" or, "No more social media!" That's the fastest way to shut the conversation down. Instead, start with: "Look, I'm not against gaming. I know it's fun. I just want you to know how to be safe while you're having fun."

That changes everything.

It's not about scaring them. It's about equipping them. And honestly, it's about staying connected, because traffickers are counting on you not being part of the conversation.

So stay in it. Ask questions. And remind your kids that their value has nothing to do with their follower count or gaming level but everything to do with who they are.

Sharenting

We can't discuss social media without discussing sharenting. What in the world is sharenting, you say? Well, that's what I said, but sharenting is a new term to explain a not-so-new practice. According to the *Oxford English Dictionary*, sharenting is defined as, "The action or practice of sharing news, images, or videos of one's children on social media websites."[15]

Rebecca Saunders of The Set Me Free Project understands sharenting all too well. I had the chance to sit down with Rebecca to discuss the topic, and she opened my eyes.

Sharenting, a blend of "sharing" and "parenting," is the practice of putting our kids online. That might mean family vlogging, running an Instagram account for a child, or even just posting "first day of school" pictures on Facebook. It sounds innocent, but the implications are much bigger than most of us realize.[16]

When Rebecca first defined the term, I immediately thought of the endless videos available on TikTok or Instagram. Just the other day, my sister sent me one of the cutest clips I had ever seen—an adorable three-year-old with a thick Southern accent announcing that her family was going out for Mexican food. I laughed out loud and thought, *This is me*. But then the reality hit me:

She was only three years old. She had no choice in that moment. Her parents had decided the world could see her.

That's the heart of the issue. Children aren't given a choice. At three years old, they can't possibly understand what it means to have their lives shared online. Frankly, even at 33 — or 53! — most of us still don't fully grasp the reach of the internet.

Rebecca pointed me to a survey from C.S. Mott Children's Hospital:[17]

- 74% of parents said they knew another parent who engages in sharenting.
- 56% said what was posted was embarrassing to the child.
- 51% admitted parents had shared details that could reveal a child's location.
- 37% had seen parents post photos that could be considered inappropriate, sometimes bath time or potty training photos that parents may see as innocent, but predators might not.

Those numbers stopped me cold.

When we post those moments we view as cute or funny, we rarely ask ourselves: *Would I want this online if it were me?* Most of us wouldn't post a picture of ourselves on the toilet, so why would we do that with our children? Kids are full people, not objects, and they have a right to privacy, even if they can't articulate it yet.

Another risk is something Rebecca called digital kidnapping, when someone takes a child's photo and pretends the child is their own. It sounds like the plot of a Lifetime movie, but it's happening in real life. Sometimes people who have lost children or want to live a different reality steal photos of kids online and build entire identities around them. Other times, predators repurpose innocent family photos in deeply disturbing ways.

And then there's identity theft. Many new parents, including Rebecca, by her own admission, share baby pictures with full names, dates of birth, and even birth weights. That's more than enough information for someone to begin building a stolen identity. The *Journal of Pediatrics* reported that 92% of U.S. children have an online presence by the age of two.[18] Two years old. Their digital footprint starts before they even know what the internet is.

I was floored by that statistic. Our kids don't create their online presence; we do. And while most parents are motivated by pride and love, the consequences can follow children for life.

I've seen this play out in real time. A good friend once posted a first day of school picture of her child. It was an adorable chalkboard sign with grade, teacher's name, school, and age. But when you think about it, that's a road map for anyone who wants to build a relationship with your child: where they go to school, how old they are, even what they're interested in.

Reminder that it's not about white vans pulling up for kidnappings. More often, it's about grooming, predators using bits of information to create false trust.

Even the National Center for Missing and Exploited Children has found that half of the images circulating among sex offenders come from social media accounts of parents—most of them fully clothed, ordinary pictures. 19

And it isn't just about strangers. Sometimes the hardest conversations come within families. I've had grandparents ask me, *"Who's right, my daughter-in-law or me? She doesn't want me posting pictures of the grandkids, but I want to show them off."* The answer? The parent is right. Boundaries must be respected. Love for a child doesn't justify risking their safety.

I'll be the first to admit this is easy to forget. Years ago, when my daughter got her learner's permit, I proudly snapped a photo of her holding it up and then posted it online. A dear friend who works in child safety called me immediately: *"Do you realize you just put your child's address out there for the world to see?"* I was mortified. I blurred it out, but the truth is, once something is out there, you can't ever guarantee it's gone

That's why Rebecca and I both stress: privacy settings aren't foolproof. Even posts you think are private can be screenshotted, shared, or hacked. And once kids are old enough, they'll have opinions about what you've shared. My son, even as a child, would tell me, *"Don't post that, Mom."* He was aware early on, and I've tried to honor that ever since.

So what can we do?

- Audit your past posts. Go back through your feeds and ask yourself: Would my child want this online when they're 16, 26, 36? If not, delete it.

- Be intentional moving forward. Ask yourself: Why am I posting this? Who benefits? Could this information be misused?

- Respect boundaries. If someone asks you not to post his or her child, don't. Period.

- Ask your own children. If they're old enough, involve them. Ask what they're comfortable with.

Social media is fun. It's creative. But it is not private. And when it comes to our children, we can't afford to confuse the two.

***

Take-home tip: Before posting about your child, try the *Front Porch Test.* Imagine your child's story being shared on your front porch for anyone passing by — extended family, acquaintances, or people you didn't intend to include. Would it still feel safe, respectful, and honoring of your child? If you pause or feel unsure, that's your cue. Some moments are meant to be protected, not posted. If not, keep it offline.

CHAPTER 4

Sexting and Sextortion

Sexting

When we talk with kids about social media, it's easy to assume they already understand the risks. After all, they're digital natives, right? But one of the most important truths we can teach our children is this: What we do online has real-life consequences. And those consequences can last far longer than any of us might imagine. This isn't just about protecting them from traffickers (although that's critical). It's also about their future opportunities, college admissions, scholarships, jobs, and relationships. Once something is shared online, they no longer under their control. Even if they delete the original post from their page, the screenshots, shares, and saves live on.

We see it all the time in the headlines. Actors lose roles, athletes are dropped from teams, and politicians are forced to resign because of something they once posted online. But this doesn't just happen to celebrities. High schoolers and college students are facing these same consequences.

Two teens once posted a racist video on TikTok and were both expelled from school. One lost her college admission. A cheerleader had her acceptance to the University of Tennessee rescinded after an old video of her saying the N-word surfaced. An Ohio senior was expelled for posting an explicit meme. And those are only a few examples.

We also need to help young people understand that it's not just what they post, it's who they follow, what they like, and what they share. Colleges and employers routinely check social media to see what someone is like when they aren't putting on a show.

So how do we guide them?

One simple tool I often recommend is what I call the *Grandma Test.* Before you post, pause and ask yourself: If Grandma saw this, or if it reached beyond the people you intended, would you still feel good about it being shared? Not because she would judge you, but because once something is online, it can travel farther than we expect. If you feel even a small hesitation, take that as your cue to reconsider before hitting "share."

Even the biggest corporations have made serious online mistakes. Take Kraft, for example. In October 2020, during the pandemic, Kraft launched a lighthearted campaign for National Noodle Day. They encouraged adults to send free noodles to friends and loved ones as a way to spread comfort, but their slogan was "Send Noods."

You can imagine how that went.

Instead of laughs, Kraft faced a flood of backlash. The hashtags #BoycottKraft and #CancelKraft started trending, and within days, the company had to pull the campaign. But here's the reality: Even though they deleted the ads, the images are still online today.

This is a perfect reminder for kids (and adults too). Once something is shared, it doesn't just disappear. We don't get to control how it spreads, how it's interpreted, or how long it sticks around.

Of course, conversations about online choices don't stop at memes and videos. One of the toughest, but also most important, conversations to have is about nudes and sexting.

The reality is this: Nudes are more common among youth than many parents realize. A 2020 survey of kids ages 9 to 12 found that 17% had shared a nude photo or video online. Among those between ages 9 and 17 who shared nudes:

- 50% sent them to someone they had never met in person
- 41% believed they were sending them to an adult
- 92% of girls who shared nudes did so not because they wanted to—but because they felt pressured to please someone else.[20]

This isn't just risky, it's dangerous. Photos can be used for blackmail, shared to humiliate, or even sold. The results can devastate young lives: lost jobs, lost friendships, reputations destroyed. Tragically, some teens have even taken their own lives after intimate photos were shared without consent.

It's vital for kids to know that being pressured to send a nude is never okay, not by a boyfriend, girlfriend, or anyone else. Every child has the right to say no in any relationship, at any time, for any reason.

And as parents and caregivers, we have to be clear. Our role is not to condemn or shame past choices. If our kids are struggling with something they've shared, they need to know that help is available, we will listen, and they're not alone.

Our goal as adults isn't to scare kids into silence but to guide them into wise choices. Simply telling them not to do it often backfires. But when we equip them with knowledge and help them think critically, they're far more likely to make decisions that protect their future.

Teaching kids how to say no

One of the most empowering lessons we can give our kids is the confidence to say no. Not just to sexting or sharing nudes but to anything that compromises their values, their safety, and/or their comfort.

The challenge is that wanting to say no and feeling safe enough to say no don't always go hand in hand. That's where we come in. We can remind them of the following:

- They always have the right to make choices in their own best interest.
- Discomfort is temporary, but online posts and photos can last forever.
- Even in a relationship, they don't owe anyone their body, their time, or their consent.

Sometimes, saying no requires creativity. I love encouraging kids to come up with fun alternatives:

- "Not today."
- "Hard pass."
- "I'm out."
- "Try again."

We can even make it into a game. See how many ways they can say no without using the actual word. The more tools they have, the easier it is to practice those boundaries in real life.

Here's the truth: Raising kids in a digital world is not easy. We can't shield them from every risk, but we *can* prepare them. We can talk openly and honestly about the permanence of online decisions. We can remind them of their value. We can equip them with tools to resist pressure. And most of all, we can create a safe place where they know they'll be heard and not judged.

Because social media and digital life are not going away. But with guidance, love, and healthy conversations, our kids can navigate them wisely, and safely.

Sextortion

Sextortion is a topic many parents would rather avoid, but it's one we cannot afford to ignore when it comes to our kids' safety. This is a word many parents may not even know, yet it's something our kids can face, sometimes without us realizing it.

Merriam-Webster Dictionary defines sextortion as this: "[a form of] extortion in which a perpetrator threatens to expose sexually compromising information (such as sexually explicit private images or videos of the victim) unless the victim meets certain demands. *Sextortion* is when an online predator tricks someone into giving them nude images or videos, and then demands money, more images, or makes other demands—threatening to share the images with the victim's friends and family if they don't comply."[21]

Sextortion happens when someone uses coercion to extort sexual images, videos, or favors from another person. They may threaten to share explicit images that already exist unless the victim complies with their demands. It's a form of blackmail, and sadly, it's becoming increasingly common among young people.

Here's the first thing every child must know: If this happens to them, it is not their fault. They didn't ask for it. They didn't deserve it. This is 100% someone else doing something wrong to them. That distinction is critical because so often our kids feel shame when they are targeted, and shame keeps them silent.

Most states now have laws against sextortion, but laws don't remove the fear and isolation that a child can feel in the middle of it. That's why giving them permission to talk about it and making sure they know they can come to another trusted adult or us is so important.

And here's another truth they need to hear, over and over again: Sextortion, nudes, or any other mistake or pressure they may face does not change their value. Their worth is not tied to what anyone else thinks, says, or does. From the moment they were born, they have been irreplaceable and of infinite value, and nothing can take that away.

As parents and caregivers, it can be tempting to lead with panic or anger when we hear words like *sextortion*, But the most powerful thing we can do is stay calm, listen, and remind our kids that they are not alone. They need to know they are loved, believed, and supported, especially if someone is trying to convince them otherwise.

***

Take-home tip: Remind your kids often that *real love never pressures*. If someone is pushing them to send a photo or text that makes them uncomfortable, that's a red flag—not a reflection of their worth.

Take-home tip: If your child is ever targeted, lead with belief and calm. The most powerful thing you can say is, "This is not your fault. We'll get through this together."

CHAPTER 5

How do I talk to my kids about this?

I often have parents ask me, "How can I talk to my kids about these topics?" Well, it begins at the beginning. What does that mean? Let me explain.

These kinds of conversations can only happen if your everyday interactions with your children are already strong. If the only time you talk to them is to criticize or scold, they won't listen. But if they know you're someone they can talk to about anything, those harder conversations will come more naturally.

For those of you with younger kids, here's a Heads-up: As they get older, they'll want to talk to you, but it'll probably be at the most inconvenient times, like 11 p.m. My kids used to come into my room late at night and say, "Hey, Mom," and I'd have to wake up and be fully present because those moments are important. Now that they're older, I still get these moments where I'll just say, "I love you guys so much," and they roll their eyes, but deep down, I know they appreciate it.

We have to build those relationships with our children because there are people who want to harm our kids and will do so by building their own relationships with them. It's all about connection, and we need to model healthy ones. For example, if we're on our phones during dinner, we're sending a message that our devices are more important than our kids. That's a dangerous precedent. We have to model for our kids that they are more important than our phones.

So let's make sure we're having those open, positive conversations with our kids, whether it's about social media, consent, or anything else, and that we're always available when they need us. This is how we protect them and keep the lines of communication open.

I said this already, but it's an important thing to say more than once. It's all about connection, and we need to model healthy ones.

***

When my daughter was in seventh grade, she and her friend were in a math class together. The teacher was the best math teacher ever. He was fun, charismatic, and good-looking. He was 35, married, and a dad of two boys. Kids loved him, and parents loved him.

When my daughter was in ninth grade, we discovered he had been arrested. He was caught sneaking into the house of my daughter's friend when her parents were out of town. It was found out that he had begun an inappropriate and illicit relationship with my daughter's friend when she was in seventh grade and 12 years old. He sexualized the relationship when she was only 13. He continued the inappropriate relationship until he was caught entering her parents' house when she was in ninth grade. He was arrested and wound up being sentenced to 30 years. It was a horrible experience for so many. He was supposed to be a trusted adult, but he wasn't.

We all have the opportunity to be safe adults for our own youth and all of the youth we might serve. But how do we become a safe adult?

Understanding trauma through a family lens

As parents and caregivers, one of the most important things we can recognize is that trauma is everywhere. In any classroom, community group, church, or family gathering, there are survivors of sexual or domestic violence. There may even be children or adults who are currently being abused or trafficked. And although it's difficult to admit, there may also be people present who intend to cause harm.

That's why understanding trauma and learning how to respond with compassion and wisdom is not optional. It's essential.

Think back to one of the most vulnerable moments in your life. What did you need from the people around you? What words were comforting? What words hurt?

I'll never forget a time when I was grieving a deep loss. People around me were trying to be helpful but often said things that were awkward or unintentionally painful. Then a friend came and simply said: "What do you need? We can talk about it, or we don't have to. We can laugh; we can cry. Whatever you need, I'm here."

That was exactly what I needed in that moment. And maybe if she had come on another day, I would have needed something different. The point is, she asked. She didn't try to fix it. She didn't tell me how to feel. She gave me space to decide what I needed. That's what trauma-informed care is all about: asking, "What do you need?" instead of assuming we already know.

What is trauma?

Trauma is more than just a hard or painful experience. It's a psychological and emotional response to something deeply distressing. And it affects each of us differently.

- **Acute trauma** comes from a one-time event, like a car accident. One child might bounce back quickly, while another may be deeply shaken for weeks or months.

- **Chronic trauma** happens when painful experiences are repeated over time, such as domestic violence or ongoing abuse.

- **Complex trauma** is layered. Human trafficking is a good example. it's not just one type of abuse but many different traumas woven together over time.

Here's the key: Trauma is trauma. What may not feel traumatic to you could be devastating to someone else. If it's traumatic for them, it's real, and we don't get to decide otherwise.

Trauma's lasting impact

Trauma can shape how a person sees themselves, how they trust others, and how they respond to stress. It can affect memory, focus, and even the body itself. Some survivors live with PTSD (post-traumatic stress disorder), which can bring flashbacks, nightmares, hyper-vigilance, and avoidance of reminders. Others may:

- Flinch or pull away from touch
- Dissociate, or mentally "check out" during stress
- Struggle with guilt, shame, or self-blame
- Seek unhealthy relationships because healthy ones feel unfamiliar or untrustworthy
- Develop somatic symptoms like headaches, stomachaches, or chronic pain
- Turn to self-harm or substance use to cope

Every person responds differently. The important thing is that we respond with care, patience, and respect.

Trauma and consent

One of the simplest yet most powerful lessons we can model is consent. For example, instead of asking someone, "Can I hug you?" which can pressure them into saying yes, we can ask, "Are you a hugger?" That gives the person space to answer honestly, without guilt. Teaching children that they have the right to say yes or no to physical touch helps protect their boundaries and reinforces their value. Consent is not just about romantic or sexual situations. It's about every interaction.

Cultural humility

Another key to being trauma-informed is cultural humility. That means being curious about who someone is, instead of assuming we already know. People from different cultures, genders, or life experiences will process trauma differently and disclose it in different ways.

When someone shares their story, we don't ask, "What's wrong with you?" Instead, we ask, "What happened to you? How can I help?

Responding to trauma disclosures

If a child or adult shares a painful experience with you, here are some guiding principles:

- **Believe the person.** Even if the story comes out in fragments or seems inconsistent, trauma memories are not always linear. They can still be true.

- **Avoid "why" questions.** "Why would you do that?" or, "Why didn't you leave?" only adds shame. Instead, ask: "How can I help?"

- **Offer choices.** Do you want to sit here or outside? Do you want to keep talking or take a break? Choices restore dignity.

- **Watch your body language.** Don't tower over the person. Get on his or her level, soften your tone, and show compassion, not pity.

- **Never make promises you can't keep.** A broken promise can feel like yet another betrayal, even if the promise was small.

- **Limit retelling.** Don't force the person to repeat the story over and over. Each retelling can retraumatize.

And perhaps most importantly, the first words out of your mouth should be: "I'm so sorry this happened to you. I believe you."

Caring for yourself

If you love or care for someone who has experienced trauma, you may begin to feel the weight of it too. This is called secondary trauma or compassion fatigue. It's real, and it matters.

That's why self-care is not selfish. It's necessary. Therapy, support systems, healthy boundaries, and rest are vital. You cannot pour into your child, your spouse, or your loved ones if you're running on empty.

The power of trauma-informed care

When we respond through a trauma-informed lens, we create spaces where people feel safe, respected, and valued. We walk alongside them instead of trying to fix them. We remind them that their stories matter, that they are believed, and that healing is possible.

As parents and caregivers, we can't shield our children from all trauma. But we *can* model healthy responses, create safe spaces, and remind them that their worth is unshakable, no matter what they've endured.

Why survivors don't always recognize their abuse

One of the questions I get asked all the time is this: "Why don't people who are being trafficked just come forward? Why don't they say they're being trafficked?"

The truth is that most people who are being trafficked don't self-identify as victims. They may not see themselves as trafficked at all. And that's not because they don't know what's happening to them. Instead, it's because of how grooming works, how trauma shapes the brain, and how shame clouds our ability to name our own experiences.

Why survivors don't self-identify

There are a few reasons for this:

- **Relationship with the trafficker.** Sometimes the trafficker is a romantic partner, a friend, or even a family member. In those cases, loyalty, fear, or love can keep someone from seeing the abuse for what it is.
- **Employment or survival needs.** Some individuals are told they are working or helping out. Teenagers, for example, may not even realize that certain jobs they're being forced into are illegal under labor laws.
- **The grooming process.** Grooming changes how people view themselves and their choices. As I noted earlier, it's important to remember that the person who goes into grooming is never the same person who comes out. Traffickers are skilled at convincing victims that what's happening is normal, consensual, or even deserved.

So when we say survivors don't self-identify, it's not that they don't know what's happening. It's that they don't recognize it as trafficking, abuse, or violence.

I'm not a trafficking survivor, but I am a survivor of sexual violence and domestic violence. From high school through my early twenties, I was assaulted multiple times. Some of those incidents were what most people would easily recognize as sexual assault. Others happened when I had been drinking and my judgment and ability to consent were compromised.

Here's the thing: I didn't call it assault. I blamed myself. I told myself it was my fault for drinking, for being in the wrong place, and for not protecting myself better. I carried that shame for years.

It wasn't until I was already doing this work, standing next to a trauma therapist in a training, that something she said hit me like a ton of bricks. I realized that what had happened to me wasn't my fault. It wasn't a bad choice. It was sexual assault. Naming it changed everything.

That's the same realization many trafficking survivors have later in life, sometimes years later. They knew what happened, but they didn't recognize what it was.

I've seen this happen in our trainings. A young person once came up to us and said, "I just realized I was trafficked by my mom." Another said, "I didn't understand that's what was happening to me until right now."

It's heartbreaking, but it's also hopeful. Awareness gives people the language they need to begin healing.

This is why we can't shy away from educating kids and adults about trafficking. Some argue, "Why tell them? Won't they figure it out on their own?" But I know firsthand that if someone had told me earlier that what happened to me wasn't my fault and was assault, I could have started healing years earlier instead of living under shame and regret.

We have discussed this already, but it is certainly worth mentioning. When I founded The Set Me Free Project, I knew that at the heart of everything we taught, we had to teach this truth: You have an intrinsic value that cannot be changed. You were born with intrinsic worth, dignity, and value that no one can take away, not by what you do and not by what's been done to you.

I didn't know that truth for a long time. I thought my choices, my shame, and my pain defined me. That belief kept me stuck. And it's the same belief that keeps so many survivors from identifying their abuse or asking for help.

When we remind survivors—whether they're children, teens, or adults—that their value cannot be changed, we're planting seeds of healing.

As parents and caregivers, we need to understand that survivors may not see themselves as victims. They may dismiss their experiences, blame themselves, or minimize the harm. Our role isn't to force them to see it differently. It's to create safe, compassionate spaces where they feel heard and valued. We may not fully understand their experience. But we can still offer love, compassion, and dignity. We can listen without judgment. And we can remind them, again and again, that they matter, that they are valuable, and that healing is possible.

CHAPTER 6

Now what? Empowerment not fear

As parents, we can blame ourselves for everything that happens to our children. The good, the bad, and the ugly. However, unless you are the one trafficking your child, it is important to recognize that you can't control the situation and that it isn't your fault if something happens.

I was talking to a mom once who shared this very thing with me. Although her daughter wasn't trafficked, she was groomed by a drug dealer who led her down a life of addiction and eventually death. This grieving mom blamed herself for years for the loss of her daughter until she finally realized it wasn't her fault.

It's important to remember that it is never the fault of the trafficked individual either. Victim blaming is something that can happen, but it is something that we cannot do. It is never someone's fault when he or she is victimized and abused.

Human trafficking is a scary subject already; we don't need to make it scarier. But it is what it is, and we need to empower each other to recognize it, respond to it, and reassure. But how do we do that as parents and caregivers? There are a couple of very important ways.

Being a trustworthy adult

For years, many of us taught our kids about stranger danger. We told them not to take candy from strangers, not to talk to someone they didn't know, and to definitely never get into a creepy white van. While well-meaning, this approach overlooked a crucial reality. It usually isn't strangers who do the most harm; instead, it's people we know.

That's why, instead of just warning kids about strangers, we need to help them learn how to recognize a trustworthy person. And we need to make sure *we ourselves* are showing up as those safe, trustworthy adults in their lives.

For some children, even family members or guardians may not be trustworthy. That makes it all the more important that we, as parents, caregivers, mentors, or educators, intentionally communicate with our kids: "I am safe. I am someone you can come to. I am ready and willing to listen."

Trust doesn't happen overnight. It's built over time through consistent words and actions. A person's job title, wealth, social media presence, or polished manners don't automatically make them trustworthy. Neither does the length of time we've known them. Trustworthiness is revealed through character, not appearances.

It's also important to remember that people can fake certain traits. Someone with harmful intentions may act kind, charming, or generous at first, only to betray that trust later. That's why actions always speak louder than words.

When it comes to being online, the rules are even more complicated. Just because someone is a friend of a friend, it doesn't mean they're safe. Online familiarity does not equal trustworthiness.

So what does it look like? At The Set Me Free Project, we teach kids—and the adults who love them—that a trustworthy person can be defined by four simple, powerful characteristics:

- **A trustworthy person will never ask you to do something illegal.** If someone pressures your child into breaking the law, even in what may be thought of as small ways, like stealing or lying, they are not trustworthy.

- **A trustworthy person will never ask you to go against your moral compass.** Kids need to know that if it feels wrong, it probably is. And anyone who encourages them to ignore that gut feeling does not have their best interest at heart.

- **A trustworthy person will never ask you to keep a secret from a parent, guardian, or another safe adult.** Secrets are one of the most common tools predators use to isolate kids. Trustworthy people don't need secrecy to build relationships. They build trust through honesty and openness.

- **A trustworthy person always wants the best for you.** This one only counts if all the others are true. If someone breaks even one of the first three rules, they cannot truly want the best for your child.

One of the most powerful things you can do for your child is to model these same trustworthy qualities in your relationship with them. When kids know they can tell you anything without fear of shaming, blame, or immediate punishment, you become the safe place that traffickers and abusers can never compete with.

We can't control every relationship our kids will have, but we can control how safe they feel with us. And that makes all the difference.

Being the adult your kids can trust

When it comes to keeping our kids safe, one of the most important things we can do is create a relationship where they know they can always come to us. Traffickers and those who mean harm thrive in secrecy. The more open the communication between you and your child, the less power those individuals have.

Here are four powerful reminders for every parent and caregiver:

Always be approachable

Your child should feel safe coming to you with anything, big or small. If they're worried you'll be too busy, too distracted, or too upset, they may hold back. That hesitation can keep them from telling you something that really matters.

Do your best not to react

This one is hard. Sometimes kids say things that make our hair stand on end. The natural reaction might be shock, anger, or fear. But if your child sees that reaction, they may shut down. Instead, take a breath and say:

"Thank you for sharing that with me."

"Tell me more about that."

There will be time for consequences or next steps later. In the moment, the most important thing is to keep that line of communication open.

Help children understand consent

Consent isn't just about relationships. It's about everyday choices. Teach your children that they always have the right to say *yes* or *no* to physical touch, conversations, or situations that make them uncomfortable. Model this by asking permission before hugs, respecting their boundaries, and talking about what healthy, mutual agreement looks like.

Know where your children are, both in the real world and online

Our kids live in two worlds: the physical one and the digital one. Knowing who they spend time with, where they hang out, what apps they're using, and who they're talking to online is a critical part of keeping them safe. This isn't about spying. It's about being present, aware, and engaged.

***

When a child discloses trauma: how to respond as a safe adult

One of the hardest, most sacred moments you may ever experience as a parent or caregiver is when a child discloses a traumatic event. It may be something that makes your heart stop, but how you respond in that moment can make the difference between a child shutting down and continuing to trust you with their truth.

Here are five key responses to keep in mind if a child shares something difficult with you:

Always believe the story.

When your child opens up, your role is not to investigate. It's to listen. Keep your body language open: kind eyes, relaxed posture, and no crossed arms. A simple, "I believe you. Thank you for telling me," can be life changing.

Remember that memories can be random.

Trauma doesn't tell its story in a neat, chronological order. Your child's story may shift or come out in pieces. That doesn't mean he or she is lying. It's simply how trauma is stored and recalled.

Avoid "why" questions.

Asking "Why did you do that?" or "Why didn't you ...?" can sound blaming. Instead, ask "What happened?" or "How did that make you feel?" And always thank them for trusting you enough to share.

Offer choices—empower them.

Trauma takes away a person's sense of control. You can give some of that back in simple ways. For example, as "Would you like to sit here or there?" "Do you want to keep talking now or later?" Even if the answer is no, honor it. That small choice matters.

Limit the number of times they retell their story.

Every retelling can reopen the wound. Respect the choice to share or not share. When professional help is needed, let the child know you'll help connect him or her to a counselor, therapist, or school support staff.

These steps can feel even harder with your own child than with anyone else's. But your calm presence, even when you're breaking inside, is what will help that child feel safe enough to heal.

And remember that your child isn't the only one who may need support. If your child discloses trauma, consider finding professional help for both of you. Their school counselor, pediatrician, or local advocacy organizations can guide you to trusted resources.

Taking care of yourself as a safe adult

Being a trustworthy adult is beautiful, but it can also be exhausting. Compassion fatigue is real. Secondary trauma is real. To remain safe for your child, you must also take care of yourself.

Some simple reminders:

- Find your own safe people to talk with.
- Practice healthy self-care routines (rest, movement, hobbies, prayer/faith, therapy)
- Remind yourself that you are not responsible for fixing everything. You are responsible for loving, listening, and guiding toward help.

Teaching kids how to respond: The READY acronym

One of the tools I love sharing with both kids and parents is the **READY acronym**. It's a simple, easy-to-remember guide that empowers kids to protect themselves in unsafe situations, whether online or in person.

R - Report anything dangerous. If something feels off, whether online or face-to-face, tell a trustworthy adult. Trust your instincts.

E – End the communication. You don't owe anyone your time or explanation. Block, hang up, or walk away.

A – Ask for help. If one person doesn't listen, keep asking until someone does. You are not alone

D – Don't engage. If the person reaches out again, ignore and exit the situation. Block online, leave in person, and seek help.

Y – Your safety first. Your safety, physical, emotional, and mental, always comes before anything else. Be your own best advocate.

***

Closing: Hope, resilience, faith, and the power of relationship

If you've read this far, you know the reality: the world our kids are growing up in is complicated. Social media, technology, vulnerabilities, predators, exploitation ... It can feel overwhelming at times. And as parents or caregivers, that weight can sit heavy on our shoulders.

But here's the truth I want you to walk away with: *There is hope.*

I've seen too many kids make wise, life-changing decisions to believe otherwise. I've seen families heal. I've seen survivors reclaim their voices and build futures full of joy. I've seen communities step up and say, "Not on our watch." Hope isn't wishful thinking. It's the anchor that tells us change is possible, one choice, one conversation, and one relationship at a time.

And hand in hand with hope comes resilience. Resilience doesn't mean never facing hardships. It means we can bend without breaking. It means we can stumble and still get back up. When our kids know they have a safe adult to turn to, when they learn how to use their voices, and when they believe deep down that they are valued and loved, that resilience becomes their shield.

I also believe in the role of faith. For me, faith has been the foundation under my feet through trauma, recovery, and rebuilding. It has reminded me that I am not defined by my past, and neither are you or your children. Faith gives us courage to move forward when fear tells us to freeze. It gives us perspective when the darkness feels overwhelming because it reminds us there is light.

And finally, the thread that ties all of these things together is relationship. Traffickers exploit through relationships—through trust twisted and manipulated. That means our greatest prevention and protection is building stronger, healthier, and more trustworthy relationships than those who mean to harm ever could. We need to build relationships where our kids feel safe to talk, know they can make mistakes and still be loved, and understand their value not because of what they do but because of who they are.

So as you close this book, here's what want you to remember: You don't have to be perfect. You just have to be present. Show up. Listen. Laugh with your kids. Ask questions. Say the awkward things anyway. Be the trustworthy adult who proves over and over again: "I see you. I hear you. I love you. You matter."

That's how prevention works. That's how healing happens. That's how we raise kids who are not only safe but strong.

Because at the end of the day, no matter the challenges ahead, you and your child have intrinsic, unshakable value. And when you lead with hope, resilience, faith, and the power of relationship, you're giving them a gift more powerful than fear. You are giving them the gift of freedom.

***

Take-home tip: Show your children you're trustworthy by keeping your promises, respecting their feelings, and being consistent in how you respond. Small actions—like following through on picking them up on time, listening without interrupting, or respecting their privacy when appropriate- send a big message: "You can count on me."

Take-home tip: Your calm, steady presence communicates more than any lecture. If kids know you'll listen without exploding, they'll keep coming back.

Take-home tip: Your first response—calm, believing, compassionate, can shape whether your children continue to trust you with their pain. Healing begins when they know they've been heard.

Parent/caregiver quick guide

Parent/caregiver quick guide: Human trafficking

Warning signs

- Sudden possession of money, hotel keys, prepaid cards, or multiple phones
- New relationships that are secretive, controlling, or significantly older
- Wearing expensive clothes, shoes, or accessories without explanation
- Talking about "making a lot of money" but not being able to explain how
- Avoiding eye contact, appearing fearful around certain adults, or hypervigilant around authorities
- Working long hours in restaurants, construction, cleaning, nail salons, agriculture, or sales crews with little or no pay
- Saying they "owe" someone something they can't pay back

What to say

- "I care more about you than about what you've done or what's been done to you."
- "If anyone is pressuring or forcing you to do something you don't want, that's not your fault."
- "You don't owe anyone your body or your labor."
- "You have value that no one can take away, no matter what."

What *not* to say

- "Why didn't you just leave?"
- "That only happens in other places, not here."
- "This is your fault for getting involved with that person."
- "You should have known better."

(Trafficking survivors often already carry misplaced shame. Judgmental language deepens that shame and shuts down disclosure.)

Where to go for help

Local resources: School counselors, youth organizations, churches, safe mentors, shelters, or domestic violence programs

Community hotlines/services: Your local police victim advocate program, social services, or crisis centers

***

Parent/caregiver quick guide: Vulnerabilities and resilience

Warning signs

- A new "friend" or relationship that seems secretive, controlling, or too good to be true
- Sudden access to expensive clothes, electronics, or money with no clear explanation
- Withdrawal from family or longtime friends; isolating behaviors
- Signs of housing instability (spending nights away, vague about where they've been)
- Heightened anxiety, depression, or self-blame
- Excessive time on social media or gaming platforms with people you don't know

What to say

- "Everyone has struggles sometimes. It doesn't make you weak, it makes you human."
- "You can always come to me, no matter what. I may not have all the answers, but I'll listen."
- "If someone is offering you things—money, a place to stay, gifts, in exchange for anything, I want to know."
- "You have unchangeable value. Nothing about what you're facing can take that away."

What *not* to say

- "This is your fault for getting into that situation."
- "You're overreacting, it's not that big of a deal."
- "Just ignore it and it'll go away."
- "You should've known better."

(These responses increase shame and isolation, which is exactly what traffickers prey on.)

Where to go for help

- Local support: School counselors, trusted teachers, youth pastors, or mentors
- Community services: Local shelters, mental health providers, or social service hotlines

***

Parent/caregiver quick guide: Building protective influences

Warning signs

- Your child feels isolated or says they "have no one to talk to."
- They withdraw from trusted adults or stop engaging in positive activities.
- They show low self-worth, saying things like "I don't matter" or "I'm not good at anything."
- They rely heavily on risky peers or online relationships for validation.
- They seem overly desperate for acceptance, approval, or love.

What to say

- "You are not your struggles; you are so much more than that."
- "Everyone has vulnerabilities, but we can also build strengths together.
- "It's okay if you don't feel strong right now; we'll find safe people and tools to help."
- "Your value doesn't change because of what you're going through."

What *not* to say

- "Why can't you be more like your brother/sister/friend?"
- "You just need to toughen up."
- "If you really tried harder, this wouldn't be a problem."
- "You shouldn't need help—you should be able to handle this."

(Kids don't choose their vulnerabilities. Shaming them only reinforces feelings of powerlessness.)

Where to go for help

- At home: Encourage open, judgment-free conversations. Set aside one-on-one time regularly.
- School counselors, coaches, mentors, faith leaders, and youth programs.
- Local support: Mental health resources, youth support centers, after-school programs, or churches.
- Crisis resources: Suicide & Crisis Lifeline: **988,** local crisis hotlines.

***

Parent/caregiver quick guide: Online consequences and digital footprints

Warning signs

- Your child deletes posts/accounts often or hides their phone when you enter the room.
- Increased anxiety after being online.
- Trouble at school tied to something posted online.
- Obsessive checking for likes/comments.

What to say

- "Once something is online, you lose control of it. How do you decide what's safe to post?"
- "I'm not here to lecture; I want to understand how you see it."
- "You are more than your likes, shares, or followers.

What *not* to say

- "You'll ruin your future if you post something dumb."
- "You kids can't be trusted with social media."
- "Hand me your phone—I'm going through everything."

Where to go for help

- School counselors or college advisors (re: digital footprints & applications)
- CyberTipline: cybertipline.org

Parent/caregiver quick guide: Sharenting

Warning signs

- Posting children's full names, schools, ages, or locations publicly.
- Sharing vulnerable moments (tantrums, bathing, potty training).
- Friends/family tagging your child without consent.

What to say

- "I want to make sure I'm respecting your privacy, are you okay with me posting this picture?"
- "Your digital footprint starts with me. I want to protect it."

What *not* to say

- "Oh, it doesn't matter—you're just a kid."
- "Everyone else shares about their kids online; it's normal."

Where to go for help

- Family sharing apps (Family Album, Google Photos, iCloud) for private memory-keeping.
- Phone app protections.

***

Parent/caregiver quick guide: Online gaming safety

Warning signs

- Spending excessive time on games, especially late at night.
- Mood changes tied directly to gaming (anger, withdrawal, anxiety).
- Secretive voice chats or sudden new "friends" online.
- Unexplained gifts (skins, credits, or money) received from others in games.

What to Say

- "Who do you usually play with online? Do you know them in real life?"

- "What do you like most about this game? What's the hardest part?"
- "It's fun to play, but your safety is always more important than winning."

What *not* to say

- "I don't care who you're talking to—just stop."
- "If you get in trouble, that's on you."
- "Games are a waste of time. Just quit."

Where to go for help

- Common Sense Media: commonsensemedia.org (parent guides to gaming apps).
- School tech specialists or family IT support for parental controls.

***

Parent/caregiver quick guide: Online predators

Warning signs

- Your child suddenly receives a lot of attention, compliments, or gifts online.

- Secretive about new friends, hiding conversations or devices.
- Dramatic changes in dress, behavior, or vocabulary linked to an online relationship.
- Talking about wanting to meet someone in person, they "met online."

What to say

- I love that you're making friends—how do you know this person?"
- "Anyone who pressures you to keep secrets isn't safe. You can always tell me."
- "If someone online makes you uncomfortable, you have the right to block them and walk away."

What *not* to say

- "Only dumb kids get tricked by predators."
- "If this happens to you, I'll take your phone away."
- "You're too smart to fall for that."

Where to go for help

- School tech specialists or family IT support for parental controls.

***

Parent/caregiver quick guide: Nudes and sexting

Warning signs

- Hiding devices or apps, especially at night.
- Sudden mood swings or panic when notifications come in.
- Receiving gifts or money from unknown sources.

What to say

- "I know this is happening with kids your age. What do you hear from your friends?"
- "If you're ever pressured, it's okay to say no, and you can always tell me."
- "No mistake can ever erase your value."

What *not* to say

- "If you ever send a nude, your life is ruined."

- "Only 'bad kids' do that."
- "I don't want to hear about it."

Where to go for help

- School counselors or local youth support groups

***

Parent/caregiver quick guide: Sextortion

Warning signs

- Child suddenly withdraws, isolates, or becomes secretive online.
- Fear of losing device access.
- Sudden unexplained requests for money/ gift cards.

What to say

- "You did nothing to cause this. It's not your fault."
- I'm so sorry this is happening to you."
- "Thank you for trusting me with this."
- "We'll get through this together. You're not alone."

Avoid: *"Why did you do that?"* or *"What were you thinking?"*—these add shame and can shut down conversation.

What *not* to say

- "Why did you send that in the first place?"
- "You've embarrassed the family.
- "You should've known better."

Warning signs

- Your child suddenly becomes very anxious or withdrawn when online. They seem fearful about losing their phone, computer, or access to certain apps.
- Large amounts of time spent deleting messages, photos, or accounts.
- Sudden requests for money, gift cards, or secrecy around finances.
- Dramatic changes in mood, shame, anger, isolation, or even talk of hopelessness.

Where to go for help

- Local law enforcement (most states now criminalize sextortion)

***

Parent/caregiver quick guide: Red flags in relationships

Warning signs

- Child's partner is controlling, jealous, or isolating them. Your child's personality changes around the partner.
- Fearful, anxious, or secretive communication.

What to say

- "I've noticed some changes. How do you feel about this relationship?"
- "You deserve to feel safe and respected in every relationship."
- "I'm here to listen, not to judge."

What *not* to say

- "I never liked them anyway."
- "Why don't you just leave?"
- "You're too young to know what love is."

Where to go for help

- Local domestic violence hotlines and advocacy centers

***

Parent/caregiver quick guide: Trauma disclosures

Warning signs

- Child begins sharing fragmented or confusing details of painful events.
- Mood swings, anxiety, or withdrawal after trying to talk.
- Repeated "testing" with small disclosures before telling more.

What to say

- "You are safe now, and I'm here for you."
- "I believe you."
- "I'm so sorry this happened to you."

What *not* to say

- "Are you sure? That doesn't sound right."
- "Why didn't you tell me sooner?"
- "Don't talk about this anymore."

Where to go for help

- School or community resources: counselor, social worker, trusted teacher, or youth pastor
- **Immediate safety concerns:** Call 911

***

Parent/caregiver quick guide: Trustworthy adults

Warning signs

- Pressures a child to keep secrets from you or other safe adults
- Asks them to do something illegal, dangerous, or harmful
- Encourages them to ignore their instincts or values

- Uses gifts, flattery, or guilt to manipulate trust
- Wants too much time alone with your child, especially in secret

What to say

- "You can always come to me if someone makes you uncomfortable."
- "If anyone asks you to keep a secret from me, that's a red flag."
- "A trustworthy person will never ask you to do something you know is wrong."
- "Your gut feeling is important; if something feels off, it probably is."
- "I want the best for you, and I'll always listen without judgment."

What *not* to say

- "Oh, they're family, you can trust them."
- "You're just being dramatic; don't worry about it."
- "But they're a teacher/coach/pastor, they wouldn't do that."
- "Stop being rude, they're just being nice."

Where to go for help

- Immediate safety concerns: Call 911
- School or community resources: counselor, social worker, trusted teacher, or youth pastor

***

Parent/caregiver quick guide: Being the adult your kids can trust

What to do

- Stay approachable—create a safe space for questions, mistakes, and hard conversations.
- Listen first, respond later. Say things like:
- *"Thank you for sharing that with me."*
- *"Tell me more about that."*
- Teach and model consent—respect their "no," and talk about healthy boundaries.

Stay involved in both their physical world (friends, activities, whereabouts) and their digital world (apps, online friends, social media use).

What not to do

- Don't overreact in the moment—it can shut down future communication.
- Don't dismiss or minimize what they share ("That's no big deal").
- Don't assume consent is implied or "automatic," always reinforce that it must be clear and mutual.
- Don't treat online life as "less real," digital choices carry real-world consequences.

Where to go for help

- School or community resources: counselor, social worker, trusted teacher, or youth pastor

***

Parent/caregiver quick guide: Responding to a disclosure

What to do

- Believe them. Say: "I'm so sorry that happened to you. I believe you."
- Keep your body language open and calm.
- Ask" what" and "how" questions instead of "why."
- Offer small choices to restore their sense of control.
- Connect them to safe, professional help.

What not to do

- Don't interrogate or push for details. Don't show shock, anger, or judgment in your face or tone.
- Don't minimize their experience ("It wasn't that bad").
- Don't make promises you may not be able to keep.

Where to go for help

- School counselor, social worker, or nurse.
- Local advocacy center or trauma-informed therapist.

National resources:

- **The Set Me Free Project:** Our website offers a *Community Resources* tab with trusted partners and links.
- National Human Trafficking Hotline: **1-888-373-7888** (or text "BEFREE" to 233733)
- National Dating Abuse Helpline: 1-866-331-9474
- NCMEC CyberTipline: cybertipline.org | 1-800-843-5678.
- FBI Internet Crimes Against Children Task Force: icactaskforce.org.
- Suicide & Crisis Lifeline: Call/Text **988** if your child feels trapped or hopeless.
- Common Sense Media: commonsensemedia.org (parent guides to gaming apps).
- National Sexual Assault Hotline (RAINN): **1-800-656-HOPE**

Reflections

1. Think about a time when you were deeply hurt or vulnerable. What words or actions from others were comforting? What responses felt hurtful or dismissive?

2. When your child is struggling, how do you typically respond? Do you tend to jump in and "fix" the problem, or do you pause to ask what they need?

3. How do you model respect for personal boundaries with your child? How might you create more space for your child to say "yes" or "no" safely?

4. Have you noticed times when your child's response seemed "bigger" than the situation? How might you respond differently if you consider that trauma could be influencing their reaction?

5. How do you care for yourself when your child's struggles feel heavy? Who is in your support system when you need encouragement or perspective?

6. How do I usually respond when my child brings up awkward or sensitive topics? Do my words and body language show that I'm a safe person to talk to?

7. How would I want someone to respond if I shared something deeply shameful or scary? Do I model that kind of response for my child?

8. What vulnerabilities might exist in my child's life right now? How can I gently strengthen protective supports around them without making them feel "less than"?

9. Who are the "safe people" in my child's life outside of me? Do they know who those people are, and do they feel comfortable reaching out to them?

10. Do I regularly talk with my child about relationships, trust, and boundaries, or do I wait until something goes wrong?

11. How do I currently show my child (in words and actions) that I am a safe and trustworthy adult? Is there one small thing I could do this week to strengthen that trust?

12. How do I usually respond when I'm surprised or scared by something my child says? Do I react with calm, or do I let my emotions show first?

13. If my child disclosed something traumatic to me tonight, what words would I want to come out of my mouth first? (Hint: "Thank you for telling me" or "I believe you" are powerful starting points.)

14. How do I show my child, through my actions, that I am approachable and safe? Is there anything I do (tone of voice, busyness, distractions) that might unintentionally shut them down?

15. Who are the trustworthy adults in my life that *I* could lean on if my child disclosed something traumatic? (School staff, faith leaders, counselors, advocacy groups, close friends/family.)

16. What am I doing to take care of myself so I can be ready for my child's hardest moments? Do I need to build in more self-care, counseling, or support for myself?

Family digital safety agreement

Because we value trust, safety, and respect in our family, we agree to the following guidelines for using technology, social media, and gaming.

1. **Respect and kindness**

- I will treat others online the way I want to be treated.
- I will not post or share hurtful, embarrassing, or shaming content about anyone, including myself.
- If I see cyberbullying or unsafe behavior, I will speak up to a trusted adult.

2. **Privacy and boundaries**

- I will not share personal information (full name, address, school, phone number, location) publicly online.
- I will ask before posting photos of friends or family.
- I understand my parents will respect my privacy but may check my accounts/devices if safety is a concern.

3. **Posting and sharing**

- Before posting, I will use the **Grandma Test**: Would I be okay if Grandma, a teacher, or my future employer saw this?
- I understand that once something is online, I lose control over it—even if I delete it.
- I will not send or request nude or sexual images.

4. **Online gaming and online Friends**

- I will only play age-appropriate games.
- I will not give personal information to people I meet through games.
- If someone makes me uncomfortable, pressures me, or asks me to keep secrets, I will tell a trusted adult.

5. **Screen time and balance**

- We agree as a family to set reasonable limits on screen use (hours on school days, hours on weekends).
- Devices will be charged/stored overnight in a family space, not in bedrooms.
- I will balance online time with sleep, family, schoolwork, and physical activity.

6. Communication and trust

- If I make a mistake online, I will talk to a parent or trusted adult instead of hiding it.
- Parents agree to respond with love and problem-solving, not shame or harsh punishment.
- Together, we will focus on learning and staying safe, not on blame.

Signatures

Child(ren):______________

Date: ____________

Parent(s)/Caregiver(s):___________

Date: _____________________

Family tech check-in

(Use this once a week, maybe at dinner or a family meeting. The goal isn't to "catch" anyone, but to keep communication open and safe.)

1. **Highs and lows**

- **Child(ren):** What was the best thing you did online this week? What was the hardest?
- **Parent(s):** Share your own highs and lows with technology this week too (model honesty!).

2. **Safety check**

- Did you see anything online this week that made you uncomfortable, upset, or pressured?
- Do you feel like you can talk to us about those things without getting in trouble?

3. **Boundaries and balance**

- How do you feel about the amount of screen time this week? Too much, not enough, or just right?
- Did our agreed screen-free times (meals, bedtime, family time) work well?

4. Relationships and respect

- Did you feel respected online this week? Did you show respect to others?
- Is there anything you need help responding to (a post, a message, a game interaction)?

5. Looking ahead

What's one way we can use tech well this coming week? (Ex: more family game nights, less late-night scrolling, sharing a funny video together.)

Bibliography

1. Meta. (2022). Meta | Social Metaverse Company. Meta | Social Metaverse Company https://about.meta.com/

2. Mac, Ryan, and Cecilia Kang. "Whistle-Blower Says Facebook "Chooses Profits over Safety."" The New York Times, 3 Oct. 2021, www.nytimes.com/2021/10/03/technology/whistle-blower-facebook-frances-haugen.html.

3. Taken. Directed by Pierre Morel, 20th Century Fox, 2008.

4. Blue Campaign. "What Is Human Trafficking?" Department of Homeland Security, Blue Campaign, 22 Sept. 2022, www.dhs.gov/blue-campaign/what-human-trafficking.

5. Shakhnazarova, Nika. "Liam Neeson Thought Iconic 'Taken' Speech Was 'Corny.'" New York Post, 22 Feb. 2023, nypost.com/2023/02/22/liam-neeson-thought-iconic-taken-speech-was-corny/. Accessed 19 Aug. 2023.

6. Tomkins, Stephen, 1968-. William Wilberforce : a Biography. Oxford :Lion, 2007.

7. United Nations. "'Only One out of 100 People Are Rescued' from Human Trafficking." UN News, 29 July 2016, news.un.org/en/audio/2016/07/615462.

8. International Labour Organization. "Annual Profits from Forced Labour Amount to US$ 236 Billion, ILO Report Finds International Labour Organization." Www.ilo.org, 19 Mar. 2024, www.ilo.org/resource/news/annual-profits-forced-labour-amount-us-236-billion-ilo-report-finds.

9. Henderson, Sarah. "Laughter and Learning: Humor Boosts Retention." Edutopia, George Lucas Educational Foundation, 31 Mar.2015, www.edutopia.org/blog/laughter-learning-humor-boosts-retention-sarah henderson.

10. Myths and Facts About Human Trafficking | The Administration for Children and Families (hhs.gov) https://www.acf.hhs.gov/otip/about/myths-facts-human-trafficking

11. "Trauma Bonding | Psychology Today." www.psychologytoday.com/us/basics/trauma-bonding.

12. Fellow, Sandra, and Urs Gasser. Teens, Social Media, and Privacy. 21 May 2013.

13. Marshall, Ethan A, and Holly A Miller. "Age and Type of First Exposure to Pornography: It Matters for Girls and Boys." Deviant Behavior, vol. 45, no. 3, 17 Aug.2023, pp. 1–17, https://doi.org/10.1080/01639625.2023.2248338.

14. Johnson, Laura, et al. Identification and Assessment of Domestic Minor Sex Trafficking (DMST). 2016.

15. Oxford English Dictionary. "Sharenting, N. Meanings, Etymology and More | Oxford English Dictionary." Oed.com, 2023, https://www.oed.com/dictionary/sharenting_n?tl=true

16. The Set Me Free Project. "The Hidden Dangers of Sharenting - Resilience & Relationships (R&R) - Stephanie Olson and Rebecca Saunders - Resilience and Relationships (R&R)." Buzzsprout, 27 Aug. 2025, resilienceandrelationships.buzzsprout.com/1862413/e the-hidden-dangers-of-sharenting-resilience-relationships-stephanie-olson and-rebecca-saunders. Accessed 16 Feb. 2026.

17. C.S. Mott Children's Hospital. "Parents on Social Media: Likes and Dislikes of Sharenting." National Poll on Children's Health, 16 Mar. 2015, mottpoll.org/reports-surveys/parents-social-media-likes-and-dislikes-sharenting.

18. Ferrara, Pietro, et al. "Online "Sharenting": The Dangers of Posting Sensitive Information about Children on Social Media." *The Journal of Pediatrics*, vol. 257, no. 113322, 17 Jan. 2023,www.jpeds.com/article/S0022-3476(23)000185/fulltext#secsectitle003, https://doi.org/10.1016/j.jpeds.2023.01.002.

19. National Center for Missing & Exploited Children. "Cyber Tipline Data." *National Center for Missing &*

Exploited Children, 2021, www.missing-kids.org/gethelpnow/cybertipline/cyber

20. Thorn. "Thorn Research: Trends Confirm Need for Parents to Talk about Online Safety with Kids Earlier, More Often." *Thorn,* 12 Nov. 2021, www.thorn.org/blog/thorn-research-trends-confirm-need-for-parents-to-talk-about-online-safety-with-kids-earlier-more-often/.

21. Merriam-Webster Dictionary. "Definition of SEXTORTION." *Www.merriam-Webster.com,* www.merriam-webster.com/dictionary/sextortion.

The Set Me Free Project

The Set Me Free Project is a nonprofit organization whose mission is to stop human trafficking before it starts by providing prevention education to people of all ages.

Its curriculum is informative, interactive, and flexible, reaching students (K–12th grade), educators, parents, and leaders across every facet of the community.

What makes The Set Me Free Project unique is its use of engaging, age-appropriate curriculum in every presentation. The organization focuses on defining human trafficking and helping students understand why and how they may be at risk. It also provides a foundation for all students to recognize the intrinsic value of every human being.

Stephanie Olson

Stephanie Olson is a speaker, an author, a podcaster, and the CEO of The Set Me Free Project.

Stephanie obtained a Bachelor of Arts degree in Psychology and a minor in English from the University of Nebraska-Lincoln. She also earned a Master of Arts in Strategic Communication from Liberty University. In addition, she possesses an Honorary Doctorate in Philosophy from TIAU Business School.

Before founding The Set Me Free Project, Stephanie worked with women in the area of sexual and domestic violence, addiction, and homelessness. She also worked with youth, teaching healthy relationships. After extensive training and research in the study of human trafficking prevention education and social media safety, she co-founded The Set Me Free Project.

Stephanie also helps leaders build resilience. Her work on teaching resilience in leadership has inspired people across the United States with topics such as, leadership, trauma, a toxic workplace, mental health, and resilience. As a woman of color and a survivor of domestic and sexual violence, Stephanie brings lived experience, research, and humor to impact lives. She is a sought-after speaker on women, youth, human trafficking, and social media safety while leading The Set Me Free Project to help prevent youth and young adults from personally experiencing trafficking.

About this book

What if you could give your children the tools to face the world with confidence, resilience, and hope—even in the face of some of life's hardest realities?

In this honest and practical guide, Stephanie Olson, CEO and Founder of *The Set Me Free Project*, invites parents and caregivers into real conversations about the risks youth face today—human trafficking, online exploitation, unhealthy relationships, and more. But this is not a book of fear. Instead, it's a book of empowerment.

With warmth, faith, and transparency, Stephanie weaves her personal story as a survivor with years of frontline experience, offering tools that are both trauma-informed and deeply relational. You'll find:

Clear explanations of tough topics like sextortion, nudes, social media safety, and vulnerabilities.

"Parent Quick Guides" with warning signs, what to say (and what not to say), and where to go for help.

Reflection questions and take-home tips to put into practice immediately.

A consistent reminder that every child has unshakable, intrinsic value—and so do you.

This book doesn't shy away from the realities our children face. But page after page, it brings you back to what makes all the difference: hope, resilience, faith, and the power of relationship.

Because prevention is not only possible, it's powerful. And with the right tools, you can be the trustworthy adult your child needs most.

Thank you for reading this book!

To learn more about The Set Me Free Project, please visit our website at:

setmefreeproject.net.

If you're interested in purchasing the companion online course, you can find more information on our website or contact us directly at info@setmefreeproject.net.

Join us in helping us STOP HUMAN TRAFFICKING BEFORE IT STARTS!®

www.ingramcontent.com/pod-product-compliance
Lightning Source LLC
LaVergne TN
LVHW010926110826
845149LV00013B/2496
* 9 7 8 0 9 9 1 4 5 4 9 2 1 *